Dependable Computer systems

ASSEN V. KRUMOV

It is known that the issue of safety and reliability of computer systems, particularly those operating as real-time control of safety critical systems becomes more and more important.

It is important also to create new scientific methods for development of safe and reliable hardware and software, which are easily applicable in practice and not only of scientific interest, as are most of the publication.

The objectives of the present book is twofold:
1. To offer a textbook for computer science students to prepare them to design in the future reliable, safe and secure computer systems as engineers.
2. To describe some new research methods, developed by the author.

The book contains also large bibliography of the latest publications in this area at the end of each chapter.

CONTENTS

3

1 INTRODUCTION.

It is known that the issue of safety and reliability of computer systems, particularly those operating as real-time control of safety critical systems becomes more and more important. Along with this, is growing the importance of the methods of training of the students of computer science to create future professionals who could carry out the design of reliable and safe computer systems for control in transport, automotive electronics, aviation, medical equipment, nuclear plants, management of banking and others.

It is important also to create new scientific methods for development of safe and reliable hardware and software, which are easily applicable in practice and not only of scientific interest, as are most of the publication.

The objectives of the present book is twofold:
1. To offer a textbook for computer science students to design in the future reliable, safe and secure computer systems as engineers.
2. To create some new research methods in this area. The book suggests the following new methods developed by the author:

a) Synthesis of combinational logic circuits with improved reliability and safety, applying the redundancy principle in this field (chapter 5).

b) Application of the fail-safe principle for the safety critical software (chapter 6).

c) A new method and algorithm for accelerated reliability testing (chapter 12).

In each chapter there is a list of articles, books and Internet sites, that readers can use for a more detailed study of the problem.

This chapter has also a list of books in the field of dependable computer systems.

REFERENCES

[1]. Miroslaw Malek, Felix Salfner, "Dependable Computing with Proactive Failure Avoidance, Recovery, and Maintenance", Springer, 2013, ISBN 978-1-4419-6453-3.

[2]. John Knight, "Fundamentals of Dependable Computing for Software Engineers", CRC Press, 2012, ISBN 9781439862551.

[3]. Rogério de Lemos, Cristina Gacek, "Architecting Dependable Systems", III-VII, Springer, 2005-2009, ISBN-13:978-3540289685.

[4]. Wojciech Zamojski, Janusz Kacprzyk, Jacek Mazurkiewicz, Jarosław Sugier, and TomaszWalkowiak, "Dependable computer systems", 2011, Springer-Verlag Berlin Heidelberg.

[5]. K. Kanoun, L. Spainhower, "Dependability Benchmarking for Computer Systems", Wiley-IEEE Press, 2008.

[6]. John R. Vacca, "Computer and information security handbook", June 5, 2009, ISBN-10: 0123743540.

[7]. J.C. Geffroy, G. Motet, "Design of Dependable Computing Systems", Springer, ISBN 978-1-4020-0437-7.

[8]. Raimund Ubar, Jaan Raik, Heinrich Theodor Vierhaus, "Design and Test Technology for Dependable Systems-on-Chip", Publisher: IGI Global; 1-st edition (December 31, 2010), ISBN-10: 1609602129, ISBN-13: 978-1609602123.

2 BASIC DEFINITIONS - DEPENDABILITY, RELIABILITY, SAFETY, SECURITY

For the computers and embedded systems, working in a real time environment, the most important characteristic is their dependability. The notion of dependability is broken down into six fundamental properties [1]:
(1) reliability;
(2) availability;
(3) safety;
(4) confidentiality;
(5) integrity;
(6) maintainability.

It is expected that a safety-critical system will be operational when needed (availability), that the system will keep operating correctly while being used (reliability), that there will be no unauthorized disclosure (confidentiality) or modification (integrity) of information that the system is using, and that operation of the system will not be dangerous (safety). Precise definitions of these terms have been developed over a period of many years by a group of researchers led by J.C. Laprie. It is important to note that security is not included explicitly in this list. Rather, it is covered by the fourth and fifth items in the list.

The most important theoretical characteristic between (1) and (6) is reliability.

2.1.Reliability

In words reliability can be described with the probability P of an item operating for a given amount of time t without failure. More generally, reliability is the capability of parts, components, equipment, products and systems to perform their required functions for desired periods of time without failure, in specified environments. Mathematically it can be described with the following equation:

$$p(t) = P(\tau \geq t), \qquad (2.1)$$

where p(t) is the function describing the probability that the system will work without failure for a time τ greater or equal to t. The probability that the system or the component will work without failure for a time τ, less than the argument t is:

$$q(t) = P(\tau < t) \qquad (2.2)$$

Obviously,

$$p(t) + q(t) = 1 \qquad (2.3)$$

The function p(t) is decreasing with the argument t (Fig.2.1a). In the first moment p(0)=1, which means that systems is in proper and correct condition and reaches zero for $t \to \infty$.

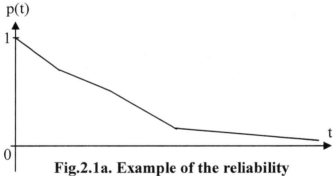

Fig.2.1a. Example of the reliability function p(t).

The function q(t) is giving the integral distribution of the failures and is called **cumulative distribution function, cdf.** The derivative:

$$f(t) = \frac{dq(t)}{dt} = -\frac{dp(t)}{dt} \qquad (2.4)$$

is called **probability density function-pdf**. The relation between them can be shown with the following example (Fig.2.1b), giving the probability of failure in the interval $t \in [a,b]$.

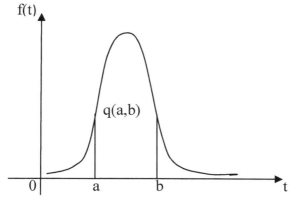

Fig.2.1b. Calculation of the probability of failure in the interval $t \in [a,b]$.

$$q\,(a,b) = \int_{a}^{b} f(t)dt \qquad (2.5)$$

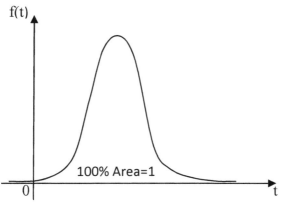

Fig.2.2 Illustration of integral (2.6).

It should also be pointed out the total area under the f(t) is always equal to 1 (Fig.2.2), or mathematically:

$$\int_{-\infty}^{+\infty} f(t)dt = 1 \qquad (2.6)$$

In the above example in Fig.2.1a, Fig.2.1b and Fig.2.2 the function f(t) is hypothetical. The most important probability density functions are that with normal distribution and exponential distribution.

2.1.1. Normal distribution

It is given analytically by (7):

$$f(t) = \frac{1}{\sigma\sqrt{2\pi}} \exp\left\{-0.5\left(\frac{t-\mu}{\sigma}\right)^2\right\}, \qquad (2.7)$$

where μ is the mean and σ is the standard deviation. The normal distribution is a two-parameter distribution, i.e. with two parameters μ and σ.

From Fig.2.3 can be seen that:

a) The mean, μ, is also the location parameter of the normal **probability density function- pdf**, as it locates the **pdf** along the abscissa. It can assume values in the interval $t \in [-\infty, +\infty]$.

b) As σ decreases, the **pdf** gets pushed toward the mean, or it becomes narrower and taller.

2.1.2. Exponential distribution

Exponential distribution is widely used for investigation of reliability in the technical and electronic fields - software and hardware. The analytical description of this distribution is:

$$f(t) = \lambda.e^{-\lambda t} = (1/m).e^{-t/m}, \ t \geq 0, \ \lambda > 0, \ m > 0, \qquad (2.8)$$

where: λ is constant failure rate, in failures per unit of measurement, *e.g* failures per hour, per cycle, etc.; $\lambda = 1/m$, where m = mean time between failures. Obviously, as $t \to \infty$, $f(t) \to 0$. Graphically this distribution is shown in the Fig.2.4.

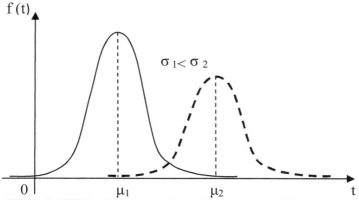
Fig.2.3. PDF of normal distribution for different σ and μ.

In the general case $\lambda(t)$ is failure rate function that describes the number of failures that can be expected to take place over a given unit of time. In many cases it can be considered to be constant. When λ is constant can be proven that $q(t) \approx t.\lambda$. Taking into account that:

$$e^x = 1 + \frac{x}{1!} + \ldots$$

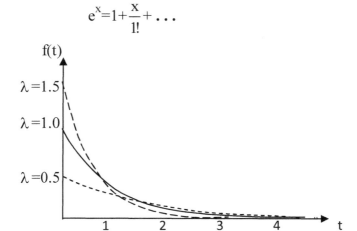
Fig.2.4. Exponential distribution

$$q(t)= \int_0^t f(t)dt = \int_0^t \lambda.\exp(-\lambda t)dt = 1 - e^{-\lambda t} \approx 1 - (1-\lambda t) \approx \lambda t,$$

the cumulative distribution function of failures is approximately:

$$q(t) \approx t.\lambda \qquad (2.9)$$

This is the reason why the requirement for safety in the railway systems and aviation are given with λ [1/h].

Typical curve of $\lambda(t)$ for electronic and computer applications is shown in Fig.2.5.

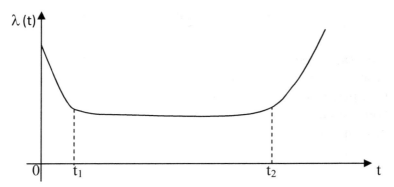

Fig.2.5. λ (t) for electronic and computer applications

It can be seen that there are 3 time intervals in Fig.2.5. The fist ($t \in [0,t_1]$) correspond to the beginning of the exploitation of the device, when the number of failure is greater, during the acceptance testing. In the second interval ($t \in [t_1,t_2]$), during the normal work λ is constant. In the third interval ($t \in [t_2,\infty]$), because of the ageing, λ increases.

2.2 Safety

In the recent years the analysis and management of hardware and software safety became one of the most important topics of the scientific research. Failures f can be divided in two: dangerous f_d and non dangerous f_n: $f = f_d + f_n$, and accordingly the probabilities for failure are: $P_f = P_d + P_n$. The reliability can be assessed by P_f and the safety- by P_d. This means that the main goal for improvement of the safety should be the reduction of the number of dangerous failures f_d and their probability P_d. Obviously the total number of failures f is greater than the number of dangerous failures f_d ($f \geq f_d$), which means that $P_f \geq P_d$. For the reduction of P_d a number of specific measures can be taken, which is the purpose of this course.

2.3.Security

Quite often failures in network based services and server systems may not be accidental or caused by incorrectness of a program, but rather caused by deliberate security intrusions. So software security can be achieved by software, which continues to function correctly under malicious attacks. Internet-enabled software applications present the most common security risk encountered today. But recently were found also malicious hardware elements, applied during the design and production of the hardware. The well known malicious software attacks include viruses, troyans, cookies, phishing, adware.

2.4.Availability

Availability is the proportion of time a system is in a functioning condition - the ratio the total time a functional unit is capable of being used during a given interval to the length of the interval. For example, a unit that is capable of being used 100 hours per week (168 hours) would have an availability of 100/168. However, typical availability values are specified in decimal (such as 0.9998).

REFERENCES

[1]. John C. Knight "Dependability of Embedded Systems", ZCSE'02, May 19-25,2002, Orlando, Florida, USA.

[2].http://www.answers.com/topic/reliability-
1#ixzz21NLkn6i1
[3].http://www.laas.fr/~kanoun/ifip_wg_10_4_sigdeb/exter
nal/02-06-25/index.html
[4].http://www.stats.gla.ac.uk/steps/glossary/alphabet.html
[5].http://www.weibull.com/knowledge/rel_glossary.htm#R

3 BASIC METHODS FOR IMPROVEMENT OF DEPENDABILITY, RELIABILITY AND SAFETY OF THE COMPUTER SYSTEMS

There are many methods for improvement of the quality of the software and hardware of the computer systems. The most important and useful are the following:

3.1.Hazard analysis

A hazard analysis is used as the first step in a process used to assess risk. The result of a hazard analysis is the identification of risks. Preliminary risk levels can be provided in the hazard analysis. The validation, more precise prediction and acceptance of risk is determined in the Risk assessment analysis. The main goal of both is to provide the best selection of means of controlling or eliminating the risk. The term is used in several engineering specialties, including avionics, chemical process safety, safety engineering, reliability engineering and food safety. An analysis or identification of the hazards which could occur at each step in the process, and a description and implementation of the measures to be taken for their control.

While in some cases safety risk can be eliminated, in most cases a certain degree of safety risk must be accepted. In order to quantify expected accident costs, the potential consequences of an accident, and the probability of occurrence must be considered. Assessment of risk is made by combining the severity of consequence with the likelihood of occurrence in a matrix. Risks that fall into the "unacceptable" category (e.g., high severity and high probability) must be mitigated by some means to reduce the level of safety risk.

IEEE STD-1228-1994 Software Safety Plans prescribes

industry best practices for conducting software safety hazard analyses to help ensure safety requirements for software that commands, controls or monitors critical functions. When software is involved in a system, the development and design assurance of that software is often governed by DO-178B. The severity of consequence identified by the hazard analysis establishes the criticality level of the software. Software criticality levels range from A to E, corresponding to severities of Catastrophic to No Safety Effect. Higher levels of rigor are required for level A and B software. Corresponding functional tasks and work products in the system safety domain are used as objective evidence of meeting safety criteria and requirements.

Severity definitions (safety related) are: catastrophic, hazardous, major, minor. Likelihood of occurrence can be: Probable - anticipated to occur one or more times during the entire system/operational life of an item with probability of occurrence per operational hour greater than 10^{-5}; Remote - probability of occurrence per operational hour is less than 10^{-5}, but greater than 10^{-7}; Extremely Remote - probability of occurrence per operational hour is less than 10^{-7}, but greater than 10^{-9}; Extremely Improbable - probability of occurrence per operational hour is less than 10^{-9}. For example the British aviation requires software failures leading to catastrophe to be less than 10^{-9} per operational hour.

3.2.Redundancy

In engineering, redundancy is the duplication of critical components or functions of a system with the intention of increasing reliability of the system, usually in the case of a backup or fail-safe.

In many safety-critical systems, such as hydraulic systems in aircraft, some parts of the control system may be triplicated, which is formally termed triple modular redundancy (TMR). An error in one component may then be out-voted by the other two. In a triply redundant system, the system has three sub components, all three of which must fail before the system fails. Since each one rarely fails, and the sub components are expected to fail independently, the probability of all three failing is calculated to be extremely small.

There are four major forms of redundancy, these are:
1. Hardware redundancy;
2. Information redundancy, such as error detection and correction methods;
3. Time redundancy, including transient fault detection methods such as Alternate Logic;
4. Software redundancy such as N-version programming.

The two functions of redundancy are passive redundancy and active redundancy. Passive redundancy uses excess capacity to reduce the impact of component failures. Eyes and ears provide working examples of passive redundancy. Vision loss in one eye does not cause blindness but depth perception is impaired. Hearing loss in one ear does not cause deafness but directionality is impaired. Performance decline is commonly associated with passive redundancy when a limited number of failures occur.

Active redundancy eliminates performance decline by monitoring performance of individual device, and this monitoring is used in voting logic. The voting logic is linked to switching that automatically reconfigures components. Electrical power distribution provides an example of active redundancy. Several power lines connect each generation facility with customers. Circuit breakers disconnect a power line when monitors detect an overload. Power is redistributed across the remaining lines.

Voting logic uses performance monitoring to determine how to reconfigure individual components so that operation continues without violating specification limitations of the overall system.

A more reliable form of voting logic involves an odd number of devices - 3 or more. All perform identical functions and the outputs are compared by the voting logic. The voting logic establishes a majority when there is a disagreement, and the majority will act to deactivate the output from other device(s) that disagree. A single fault will not interrupt normal operation. This technique is used with avionics systems, such as those responsible for operation of the space shuttle.

Each duplicate component added to the system decreases the probability of system failure according to the formula:

$$Q(t) = \prod_{j=1}^{m} q_j(t) \qquad (3.1)$$

where: m - number of components; q_j - probability of component j failing; $Q(t)$ - the probability of all components failing (system failure). This formula assumes independence of failure events. That means that the probability of a component B failing given that a component A has already failed is the same as that of B failing when A has not failed. There are situations where this is unreasonable, such as using two power supplies connected to the same socket, whereby if one power supply failed, the other would too.

3.3. Fault-tolerance

In engineering, fault-tolerant design is a design that enables a system to continue operation, possibly at a reduced level, rather than failing completely, when some part of the system fails. The term is most commonly used to describe computer-based systems designed to continue more or less fully operational with, perhaps, a reduction in throughput or an increase in response time in the event of some partial failure. That is, the system as a whole is not stopped due to problems either in the hardware or the software.

The fault-tolerance can be achieved applying redundancy. However providing fault-tolerant design for every component is normally not an option. In such cases the following criteria may be used to determine which components should be fault-tolerant:

1. How critical is the component?
2. How likely is the component to fail?
3. How expensive is it to make the component fault-tolerant?

Fault-tolerance is not just a property of individual machines; it may also characterize the rules by which they interact. For example, the Transmission Control Protocol (TCP) is designed to allow reliable two-way communication in a packet-switched network, even in the presence of communications links which are imperfect or overloaded.

The basic characteristics of fault tolerance require:

1. If a system experiences a failure, it must continue to operate without interruption during the repair process.
2. Fault isolation to the failing component - when a failure occurs, the system must be able to isolate the failure to the offending component.
3. Fault containment to prevent propagation of the failure - some failure mechanisms can cause a system to fail by propagating the failure to the rest of the system and cause overall system failure. Mechanisms that isolate the failing component to protect the system are required.

On analogy in the internet applications the term intrusion-tolerance is introduced concerning the work of the computer system under malware attack.

3.4. Fail-safe

A fail-safe device is one that, in the event of failure, responds in a way that will cause no harm, or at least a minimum of harm, to other devices or danger to personnel.

A system's being "fail-safe" means not that failure is impossible/improbable, but rather that the system's design prevents unsafe consequences of the system's failure; that is, if and when a "fail-safe" system "fails", it is "safe" or at least no less safe than when it is operating correctly.

Examples:

1. Air brakes on railway trains and air brakes on trucks. The brakes are held in the "off" position by air pressure created in the brake system. Should a brake line split, or a carriage become de-coupled, the air pressure will be lost and the brakes applied. It is impossible to drive a train or truck with a serious leak in the air brake system.

2. A railway semaphore signal is designed so that should the cable controlling the signal breaks, the light returns to the "red" position, preventing any trains passing the inoperative signal.

3. The automatic protection of programs and/or processing systems when a computer hardware or software failure is detected in a computer system.

4. In railway signals which are not in active use for a train are required to be kept in the "danger" position. The default position of every signal is therefore "danger".

3.5. Multiple programming

N-version programming (NVP), also known as multiversion programming, is a method or process in software engineering, where multiple functionally equivalent programs are independently generated from the same initial specifications. The concept of N-version programming was introduced in 1977 by Liming Chen and Algirdas Avizienis with the idea that the "independence of programming efforts will greatly reduce the probability of identical software faults occurring in two or more versions of the program". The aim of NVP is to improve the reliability of software operation by building in fault tolerance or redundancy.

The general steps of N-version programming are:

1. An initial specification of the intended functionality of the software is developed. The specification should unambiguously define: functions, data formats (which include comparison vectors, comparison status indicators), cross-check points, comparison algorithm, and responses to the comparison algorithm.

2. From the specifications, two or more versions of the program are independently developed, each by a group that does not interact with the others. The implementations of these functionally equivalent programs use different algorithms and programming languages. At various points of the program, special mechanisms are built into the software, which allow the program to be governed by the N-version execution environment (NVX). These special mechanisms include: comparison vectors, comparison status indicators, and synchronization mechanisms. The resulting programs are called N-version software (NVS).

3. Some N-version execution environment (NVX) is developed which runs the N-version software and makes final decisions of the N-version programs as a whole, given the output of each individual N-version program. The implementation of the decision algorithms can vary ranging from simple as accepting the most frequently occurring output (for instance, if a majority of versions agree on some output, then it is likely to be correct) to some more complex algorithm.

Researchers have argued that different programming teams can make similar mistakes. When in 1986, Knight & Leveson conducted an experiment to evaluate the assumption of independence in NVP, they found that the assumption of independence of failures in N-version programs failed statistically.

N-version programming has been applied to software in railway control, performing flight control computations on modern airliners, electronic voting.

3.6. Hardware testing

Automated Test Equipment (ATE) is any apparatus that performs tests on a device, using automation to quickly perform measurements and evaluate the test results. An ATE can be a simple computer controlled digital multimeter, or a complicated system containing dozens of complex test instruments, capable of automatically testing and diagnosing faults in sophisticated electronic packaged parts or on wafer testing, including System-On-Chips and Integrated Circuits.

Diagnostic design specification is a document indicating how the diagnostics will be implemented on an upcoming/new products that will be developed by the company. It describes the behavior of the diagnostics like how the test will execute, how the output messages are formatted, and how the final result is displayed.

A hardware test engineer is a professional who determines how to create a process that would test a particular product in manufacturing, quality assurance or related area, in order to assure that the product meets applicable specifications.

3.7. Software testing

Software testing is an investigation conducted to provide with information about the quality of the product or service under test. Test techniques include the process of executing a program with the intent of finding software bugs (errors or other defects). Software testing can be stated as the process of validating and verifying that a software program /application/ product: a) meets the requirements that guided its design and development described in the specification; b) works as expected.

Software testing, depending on the testing method employed, can be implemented at any time in the development process. Traditionally most of the test effort occurs after the requirements have been defined and the coding process has been completed. Testing cannot establish that a product functions properly under all conditions, but can only establish that it does not function properly under specific conditions. A testing organization may be separate from the development team.

Not all software defects are caused by coding errors. One common source of expensive defects is caused by requirement gaps, e.g., unrecognized requirements of the specification, that result in errors of omission by the program designer.

A very fundamental problem with software testing is that testing under all combinations of inputs and preconditions (initial state) is not feasible, even with a simple product. That is why hazard analysis should identify the software modules, where the bugs can be potentially dangerous in the safety critical systems and their test should be performed for almost all combinations of inputs (input vectors).

A study conducted in 2002 reports that software bugs cost the U.S. economy $59.5 billion annually.

There are many methods for software testing, which will be described later.

3.8. Fault tree analysis

Fault tree analysis (FTA) is deductive failure analysis in which an undesired state of a system is analyzed using boolean logic to combine a series of lower-level events. This analysis method is mainly used in the field of safety engineering and reliability engineering to determine the probability of a safety accident or a particular system level failure.

An undesired effect is taken as the root ('top event') of a tree of logic. Then, each situation that could cause that effect is added to the tree as a series of logic expressions. When fault trees are labeled with actual failure probabilities of its elements, failure probabilities of the system (or

23

subsystem) can be calculated from fault trees. The Tree is usually written out using conventional logic gate symbols-Fig.3.1.

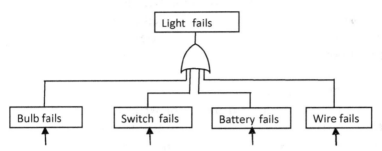

Fig.3.1. Simple example of the fault tree diagram [16].

REFERENCES

[1]. http://en.wikipedia.org/wiki/Hazard
[2]. http://en.wikipedia.org/wiki/Redundancy
[3]. http://en.wikipedia.org/wiki/Fault-tolerant_design
[4]. http://en.wikipedia.org/wiki/Fault-tolerant_system
[5]. http://en.wikipedia.org/wiki/Fail-safe
[6]. http://en.wikipedia.org/wiki/N-version_programming
[7]. http://en.wikipedia.org/wiki/Category-Hardware_testing
[8]. http://en.wikipedia.org/wiki/Automatic_test_equipment
[9]. http://en.wikipedia.org/wiki/Diagnostic_design_specification
[10].http://en.wikipedia.org/wiki/Software_testing
[11].http://en.wikipedia.org/wiki/Test_engineer
[12].http://www.weibull.com/basics/fault-tree/index.htm
[13].http://en.wikipedia.org/wiki/Fault-tree_analysis
[14].http://en.wikipedia.org/wiki/Failure_mode_and_effect_analysis

4 MODELS OF HARDWARE RELIABILITY. CALCULATION OF RELIABILITY FOR DIFFERENT HARDWARE MODELS

Each computer system consists of many different parts, components, equipment, characterized with their own reliability. It is necessary to determine the probability of work without failure of the computer system as a whole, taking into account the probability characteristics of the different components of the system.

For the calculation of reliability the multiplication rule is widely used. It determines the probability that two events, A and B, both occur. For independent events (that is events which have no influence on one another) the rule is:

$$P(A \text{ and } B) = P(A).P(B) \qquad (4.1)$$

There a different models of the computer systems, consisting of separate parts and components and accordingly – different formulas for the calculation of reliability.

4.1. Sequential model

Graphically this model is shown in Fig.4.1.

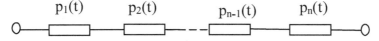

Fig.4.1 Sequential model of reliability

The probability of work without failure $P(t)$ of the computer system for this model is calculated as product of corresponding probabilities $p_i(t)$ of the different components of the system:

$$P(t) = \prod_{i=1}^{n} p_i(t) \qquad (4.2)$$

The formula (4.2) means that for the failure of the whole systems is enough only one of the components to fail.

Example 4.1: Let us consider a computer system with 1 processor, 1 memory board, 1 disk drive and 1 printer. The probability to work without failure for 1 year for each of them is $p_i=0.9$. Then the probability that the computer system as a whole will work without failure during 1 year is $P= (0.9)^4 \approx 0.66$, which is much less than the probability for the same period of each component. This means that this model should not be applied in the important cases.

4.2. Parallel model

Graphically this model is shown in Fig.4. 2.

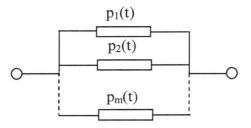

Fig.4.2. Parallel model of reliability

This model can be applied in the case when in the computer system there are many devices with identical or similar function and the failure of the system will occur when all of them fail. In this case multiplication rule will be applied for the probabilities of f failure of the different **independent** devices $q_j(t)=[1- p_j(t)]$ to calculate the probability of failure of system Q(t):

$$Q(t) = \prod_{j=1}^{m} [1 - p_j(t)] \qquad (4.3)$$

The reliability in this case is:

$$P(t) = 1 - Q(t) = 1 - \prod_{j=1}^{m} [1 - p_j(t)] \qquad (4.4)$$

Example 2: Let us consider a computer system with 4 disk drives. The probability to work for 1 year without failure is 0.9 for each of them. If can be accepted that he computer system is able to work with only 1 disk drive, then the probability, that the disk subsystem will not fail is:

$$P = 1 - [1 - 0.9]^4 = 1 - [0.1]^4 = 1 - 0.0001 = 0.9999$$

Obviously this model gives much better result than the previous sequential model.

4.3. Mixed model

Graphically this model is shown in Fig.4.3.

This model correspond to the case when the computer system consist of n groups of different devices and each group has mi(i=1,2,...n) functionally analogical devices. Failure of the whole computer system will occur when all devices in any group fail. Probability this to happen is:

$$P(t) = \prod_{i=1}^{n} \left\{ 1 - \prod_{j=1}^{mi} [1 - p_{ij}(t)] \right\} , \qquad (4.5)$$

where $\prod_{j=1}^{mi} [1 - p_{ij}(t)]$ is the probability of failure Q_i of the devices of group i. For example the computer system can have m1 processors, m2 disk drives, m3 printers, m4 terminals, m5 memory boards, m6 magnetic tape drives. The system can work, of cause not in optimal regime, if at least 1 device of each group can function.

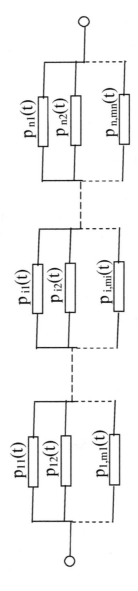

Fig.4.3. Mixed model of reliability

28

4.4. Redundancy models

In engineering, redundancy is the duplication of critical components or functions of a system with the intention of increasing its reliability. Two methods of redundancy can be applied for the hardware of the computer systems.

1. General redundancy. In this method the whole computer system is automatically replaced if the real time diagnostic detected failure, according to Fig.4.4.

Each parallel branch in Fig.4.4 corresponds to a separate computer system, the reliability of which can be calculated applying formula (4.2). The reliability of the whole redundancy model, if m computer systems connected in parallel are identical, can be determined applying formula (4.4) for the parallel model:

$$P(t) = 1 - Q(t) = 1 - (1-P_j)^m = 1 - [1 - \prod_{i=1}^{n} p_i(t)]^m \qquad (4.6)$$

where $\prod_{i=1}^{n} p_i(t)$ is the reliability of one of the parallel working systems.

2. Separate redundancy. This model coincide with the mixed model if m_i = const. It can be proven [1] that the relation between probabilities of failure of the general Qgen and separate Qsep redundancy is:

$$\frac{Qgen}{Qsep} \approx n^{(m-1)} , \qquad (4.7)$$

where m is the number of parallel branches or computers and n – number of devices with different functions. It can be concluded that for n>1, m>1 the probability of failure Q is greater for the general redundancy.

3. Majority redundancy model. The control circuit in this case is shown in Fig.4.5. It includes N computers and majoritarian device. It defines which computer system to be excluded in the case of failure of some of them.

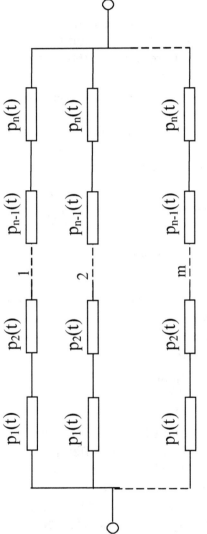

Fig.4.4. General redundancy model

30

If K computers have the same output control signal or output data and K>N/2, then they can be considered as correct signal or data. For example the American space shuttle has 5 computers and it can fly if the output of 3 of them coincide.

The discrepancy of this method is that the majoritarian device has its own probability of failure, which is not zero.

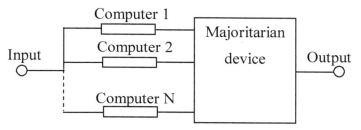

Fig.4.5. Majority redundancy model

REFERENCES

[1]. D. Arnaudov, A. Krumov, "Computer science"/in Bulgarian/, Published by VVTU "T. Kableshkov", 1989, Sofia.

5 SYNTHESIS OF COMBINATIONAL LOGIC CIRCUITS WITH IMPROVED RELIABILITY AND SAFETY

5.1. Introduction

In many cases a significant part of the safety critical embedded systems consist of logical circuits, which can be part of ASIC (Application Specific Integrated Circuit), part of SOC (System on a Chip) or can consist of standard logical circuits (TTL, HCMOS, CMOS). Sometimes when there is no need of intelligent control it is wise to use logical circuits instead of microprocessors, because their failure rate is lower then the failure rate of the microprocessors- Table 5.1 [1]. Nevertheless the reliability of the complex logical circuits, consisting of many logical elements is not high enough for the safety critical applications in the transport, medical equipment etc. and measures should be taken to improve their reliability and especially - to reduce the probability of potentially dangerous failures.

This problem is solved in [3] applying specific redundancy method for: a) 2 of 3 complex logical circuits L.C.; b) 3 of 4 logical circuits L.C.; and applying also standard logical IC of the 74xx family. The mathematical calculations of the probability of failures show big improvement of the safety while the reliability is also improved. In the both cases a) and b) the safety depends mainly on the reliability of the final element with logical function "AND", the failure rate of which for the present moment can be expected to be [1,2] $\lambda = 10^{-9}$ [failure/hour], for the standard logical IC, which in the most cases is satisfactory [4].

Table 5.1. Failure rates of IC and microprocessors

Type of IC	Function	λ [10^{-9} failure/hour]
74LS00	4 elements "NO AND"	10
2764	EPROM	9400
8085	8 bit microprocessor	190
8086	16 bit microprocessor	990

5.2.Theoretical background and assumptions

In the paper the calculations of the probabilities are made assuming that the failures of the logical circuits L.C. of which consist the redundancy model and the other IC in the configuration of the model are independent. This is true if they are not on the same chip and is partly true if they are on one chip, depending on the type of defect and taking into account that "catastrophic defect that prevent the circuit from functioning at all are rare" [5]. Nevertheless for very important safety critical systems the redundancy method should not be applied on one chip.

In the paper the failures of the L.C. and IC are considered symmetrical, i.e. the probabilities of erroneous logical outputs "1" and "0" are equal. It is assumed that the erroneous logical "1" output is potentially dangerous, while the erroneous "0" output affects only the reliability and not the safety of the system. For example "1" can switch on erroneously the green light on the semaphore, while an erroneous "0 " - the read light.

The calculations of the of the probabilities of failures are performed in the paper using the formulas [7,6]:

$$P\{A \text{ OR } B\} = P\{A\} + P\{B\} - P\{A\}.P\{B\} \leq$$
$$\leq P\{A] + P\{B\} \tag{5.1a}$$
$$P\{E_1 \text{ OR } E_2 \text{ OR } E_3 \text{ OR } E_4 \text{ OR } E_5\} \leq$$
$$\leq P\{E_1\} + P\{E_2\} + P\{E_3\} + P\{E_4\} + P\{E_5\}, \tag{5.1b}$$

where equality corresponds to the case when the events E_1, E_2, E_3, E_4, E_5 are incompatible, which is the worst case. For the case under consideration $P\{E_i\} = Q_i$ (probability of failure) and the worst case coincides with the real case because $P\{E_1\}$, $P\{E_2\}$, $P\{E_3\}$, $P\{E_4\}$, $P\{E_5\}$ have very small values and their product is even smaller. The probability of failure can be estimated taking into account (2.9) that $Q(t) \approx \lambda.t$ if $\lambda t \ll 1$ and $\lambda = $ const.

5.3. System configuration with redundancy 2 of 3

A system configuration is suggested and shown in fig.5.2 with redundancy 2 of 3 for the complex logical circuit L.C. (or microprocessor, computer) with insufficient reliability. The input logical signals to the three identical L.C. are $x_1,..x_n$ and the logical output signal are k_1, k_2, k_3. Of cause the logical values of k_1, k_2 and k_3 will coincide if the three identical L.C. work correctly without failures. In the case when 2 of the 3 identical L.C. have output signal logical "1" , the output signal of the configuration 2 of 3 will also be considered equal to "1". In all other cases of lack of coincidence (or all output signals are "0") the output signal will be considered equal to "0". This corresponds to the truth Table 5.2, the Carnot chart shown in fig.5.1 and to the analytical expression in (5.2):

$$Y = k_1.k_2 + k_2.k_3 + k_1.k_3 \tag{5.2}$$

This analytical form can be implemented using the logical IC 7452 (Fig.5.3), the analytical form (Boolean function) of which is:

$$Y_{52} = x_A.x_B + x_C x_D x_E + x_F.x_G + x_H.x_I \tag{5.3}$$

Table 5.2. Truth table for redundancy 2 of 3

k_1	k_2	k_3	Y
0	0	0	0
0	0	1	0
0	1	0	0
0	1	1	1
1	0	0	0
1	0	1	1
1	1	0	1
1	1	1	1

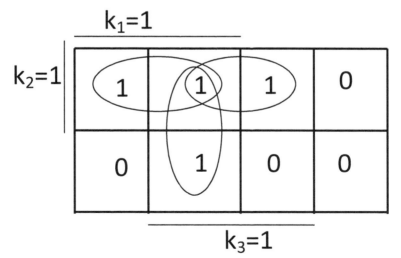

Fig.5.1. Carnot chart for redundancy 2 of 3

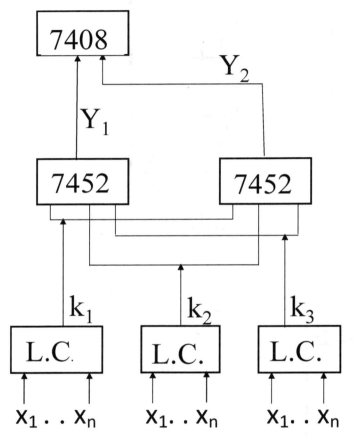

Fig.5.2.Control system configuration with redundancy 2 of 3

The Boolean function (5.3) is more general form than (5.2) and it is not difficult to be converted into (5.2) if x_i is replaced appropriately with k_j.

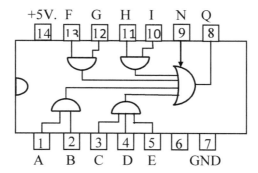

Fig.5.3 Logical IC 7452

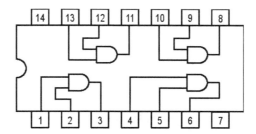

Fig.5.4 Logical IC 7408

The IC 7452 is relatively complex circuit and it can be expected, that its reliability is not high enough. That's the reason why two IC 7452 are used and their outputs Y_1 and Y_2 are multiplied logically with IC 7408 (Fig.5.4). When they does not coincide, the output control signal will be "0", which corresponds to a safe state of the system under control.

The reliability of the final logical element "AND" in Fig.5.2 **is decisive for the safety and reliability** of the whole system and its chip must be carefully chosen between the leading world producers of IC with high reliability. The IC can be 7408 or 74LS00 ("NOT AND"), if a second logical element in the chip is used as inverter.

In some specific applications, when there are two consequent executive devices (switching off or signaling when the system is not in a safe state) and the output control signals Y_1 and Y_2 can be send to the two executive devices independently , the IC "AND " can be eliminated and as result, the safety and reliability - increased.

5.3.1. Determination of the probability of dangerous failure

The determination of the probability of dangerous failure Q_{DAN} can be performed taking into account that dangerous is the failure, the result of which is an erroneous logical "1" as output. This can be consequence according to formula (5.1b) of one of the following failures of the logical IC (for the worst case):

a) failure of 2 or 3 of the L.C. - $(0.5Q_{LC})^3 + 3(0.5Q_{LC})^2$;
b) failure of the both 7452 - $(0.5Q_{52})^2$;
c) failure of 7408 - $0.5Q_{08}$.

Applying formula (1) the result is:
$$Q_{DAN} = (0.5Q_{LC})^3 + 3(0.5Q_{LC})^2 + (0.5Q_{52})^2 + 0.5Q_{08} \quad (5.4)$$
Taking into account that the values of the probabilities of failure in (5.4) are much less then 1, decisive for the value of Q_{DAN} are $3(0.5Q_{LC})^2$ and $0.5Q_{08}$:
$$Q_{DAN} \approx 3(0.5Q_{LC})^2 + 0.5Q_{08} \quad (5.5)$$
Obviously it is assumed that the probabilities of failure of IC 7452, 7408 are lower than Q_{LC} (or microprocessors- Table 5.1) and are neglected , when they are to the power of 2 or multiplied. It can be expected that
$$(0.5Q_{52})^2 << 3(0.5Q_{LC})^2, \quad (5.6)$$
because 7452 is much simpler circuit than microprocessors and complex L.C.(microprocessors).

The coefficient 0.5 in the above formulas corresponds to

the assumption of symmetry of the failures.

The conclusion is that if the logical "AND" IC is carefully chosen and is with high enough reliability, then the probability of dangerous failure of the system Q_{DAN} will depend on the value of Q_{LC} to the power of two or Q_{08}, which means significant reduction of Q_{DAN}.

5.5.2 Determination of the probability of failure (dangerous and non dangerous)

On analogy with the previous paragraph the probability of any failure (dangerous - erroneous logical "1" and non-dangerous - erroneous logical "0") of the system can be determined (for the worst case) as result of one of the following failures:

a) failure of 2 or 3 of the L.C. - $(Q_{LC})^3 + 3(Q_{LC})^2$;
b) failure of the both 7452 - $(Q_{52})^2$;
c) failure of one of the two 7452 (erroneous "0") - $2Q_{52}(0.5)$
d) failure of 7408 - Q_{08}.

Applying formula (5.1b) for this case the probability of failure is obtained:

$$Q = (Q_{LC})^3 + 3(Q_{LC})^2 + (Q_{52})^2 + 2Q_{52}(0.5) + Q_{08} \approx$$
$$\approx 3(Q_{LC})^2 + Q_{52} + Q_{08} \qquad (5.7)$$

It can be expected that the obtained probability Q will be in most cases less then the probability of failure of the logical circuit Q_{LC}(or microprocessor), because Q depend mainly on the reliability of relatively simple IC- 7452, 7408.

5.6. System configuration with redundancy 3 of 4

In Fig.5.5 Carnot chart for the case of redundancy 3 of 4 is shown. When 2 of the 4 identical L.C. are with output "1" and the other 2 with output "0" , then logical "0" is assumed as common output. The analytical form in this case is:

$$Y = k_1.k_2.k_3 + k_1.k_2.k_4 + k_1.k_3.k_4 + k_2.k_3.k_4 , \qquad (5.8)$$

which can be implemented with the IC 7452 and 7408 applying the substitutions:

$x_C=x_A=k_1, x_G=x_B=k_2.k_3, x_F=k_4, x_H=k_1.k_4, x_I=k_3, x_D=k_2,$
$$x_E=k_4 \qquad (5.9)$$

The logical products $k_2.k_3$ and $k_1.k_4$ are obtained from the IC 7408 and are send to the proper input of 7452 , in accordance with (5.8), (5.9). In 7408 two logical elements remain unused. For a configuration analogical to the shown in Fig.5.2, the probabilities of failures will be as follows:

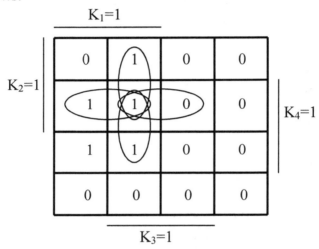

Fig.5.5. System configuration with redundancy 3 of 4

5.6.1 Determination of the probability of dangerous failure

Dangerous failure will happen if :
a) failure of 3 or 4 of the L.C. - $(0.5Q_{LC})^4 + 4(0.5Q_{LC})^3$;
b) applying (5.1a) for the failure of the double application of 7452, 7408 in (5.8), (5.9) - $0.5^2(Q_{52}+Q_{08})^2$;
c) failure of 7408 - $0.5Q_{08}$.
$Q_{DAN}= (0.5Q_{LC})^4 + 4(0.5Q_{LC})^3 + 0.5^2(Q_{52}+Q_{08})^2 +0.5Q_{08} \approx$
$\approx 0.5(Q_{LC})^3 + 0.5Q_{08}$ \qquad (5.10)
Obviously the result (5.10) is better than (5.5) especially

for the case when the LC are with low reliability. It is assumed that the probabilities of failures of IC 7452, 7408 , are lower than Q_{LC} and are neglected , when they are to the power 2 or multiplied.

5.6.2. Determination of the probability of failure (dangerous and non dangerous)

Applying analogy with the configuration shown in Fig.5.2, failure (dangerous and non dangerous) can happen if:

a) failure of 3 or 4 of the L.C. - $(Q_{LC})^4 + 4(Q_{LC})^3$;

b) failure of the both (7452, 7408) - $(Q_{52}+Q_{08})^2$;

c) failure of one of the two (7452, 7408) (erroneous "0") - $2(Q_{52} + Q_{08}) (0.5)$;

d) failure of 7408 - Q_{08}.

The probability of failure in this case is:

$$Q = Q_{LC}{}^4 + 4(Q_{LC})^3 + (Q_{52}+Q_{08})^2 + (Q_{52} + Q_{08}) + Q_{08} \approx$$
$$\approx 4(Q_{LC})^3 + Q_{52} + 2Q_{08} \qquad (5.11)$$

The obtained result is better then (5.7) especially concerning L.C. with low reliability, if $Q_{LC} > Q_{52}$.

CONCLUSIONS

1. In this chapter the method of redundancy is applied using standard logical circuits.

2. The suggested configurations of logical circuits decrease significantly the probability of dangerous failure and also in some extent - the probability of failure.

3. The method can be applied for control of safety critical systems with complex logical circuits LC, or microprocessors and computers, reliability of which are not high enough (Table 5.1).

4. It can be expected that safety (and in most cases reliability) of the suggested configurations will be much higher then that of microprocessor based systems.

REFERENCES

[1]. Palo Sauli "Reliability Prediction Of Microcircuits",

Microelectron. Reliability, vol.23, No.2, pp.283-294, 1983.

[2]. P. Brambilla , F. Fantini ,G. Mattana" Updating of CMOS Reliability", Microelectron. Reliability, vol 23, No. 4, pp.761-765, 1983.

[3]. A.Krumov "Safe and fault-tolerant control with logical circuits", Proceedings of the IEEE Conference on Control Applications, June 23-25, 2003, Istanbul, Turkey, vol.2, pp.1387-1389.

[4]. Bernard de Neumann " Software certification", Elsevier Applied Science, UK, 1988.

[5] .W.M. Needham "Nanometer technology challenges for test and test equipment", Computer, magazine, November 1999, pp. 52-57.

[6]. G. Corn , T. Corn " Mathematical handbook ", second edition, McGraw-Hill Book Company,1968.

[7]. B.V. Gnedenco, A. Hinchin " Elementary introduction to the reliability theory"(in Russian), "Nauka ", 1970, Moscow.

6 STRUCTURAL MODEL AND CHARACTERISTICS OF SOFTWARE RELIABILITY AND SAFETY

6.1. Introduction

In the scientific papers a lot of different models [1] of reliability and safety of the software, based on statistical data and various hypothesis exist, but the results obtained by the different researchers are contradictory. For example while most of them represent [2] the function of the failure rate as decreasing , in [3] it is shown as increasing linear function of the time. The main reason for these contradictions is that the software product has only one exploitation life, i.e. one test result from the practice, which is not enough for statistical interpretation and conclusions. That's why in this chapter the function of the distribution of failures and failure rate $\lambda(t)$ are connected with the structure of the program module, the input vector distribution and the verification tests, carried out with the modules of the software.

6.2. Structural model of software reliability

6.2.1. Structure of the software module and input vector distribution

It will be considered further , that the program is with modular organization and according to the principles of the structural programming with no operators GOTO backwards. Without loss of generality the analysis will be maid for an exemplary software module shown in Fig.6.1, where the conditional operators are indicated with rhombuses and it is considered, that between them different types of operators or blocks or even modules of lower level exist.

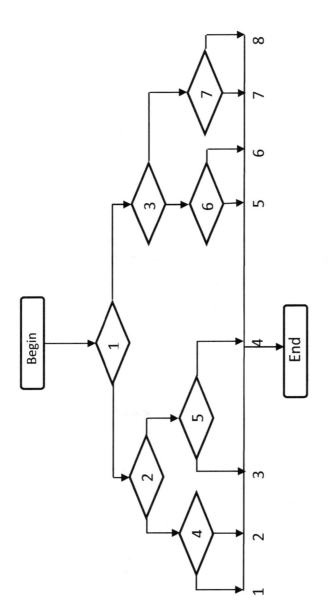

Fig.6.1.The structure of an exemplary software module

44

The input data are set A of vectors $\mathbf{a}(\mathbf{a} \in A)$ and each sequence i of execution of conditional operators (for the example in Fig.6.1 (i=1,...8) correspond to a set A_i of the vectors $\mathbf{a_i}$:

$$A = A_1 + A_2 + \ldots A_i + \ldots + A_m, \quad i=1,\ldots m, \quad \mathbf{a_i} \in A_i \qquad (6.1)$$

When the input data are discrete A_i is finite:

$$A_i = (\mathbf{a_{i1}, a_{i2}, \ldots a_{ik}}), \qquad (6.2)$$

where k is finite. However in the general case the set A_i is infinite.

The probability P_i that the algorithm will be executed in sequence i, i.e. the input vector belongs to the subset A_i forms a discrete distribution , where obviously:

$$\sum_{i=1}^{m} P_i = 1 \qquad (6.3)$$

If the probabilities P_i are multiplied by the probabilities of failure K_i during the execution of sequence of operators i , the exemplary discrete distribution of the probabilities of failure shown in Fig.6.2 will be obtained. For this distribution the following relation for one execution of the algorithm can be written:

$$P_f = P_{failure} = \sum_{i=1}^{m} P_i.K_i < 1 \qquad (6.4)$$

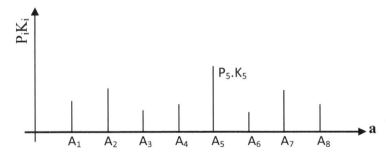

Fig. 6.2. An exemplary distribution of
probabilities of failure

45

The concrete values of the probabilities K_i depend mainly on the quantity and quality of the tests carried out for the sequence of operators i.

6.2.2. A two dimentional distribution of the probability of failure

If the sequence of operators i is thoroughly tested for a number of vectors $a_i \in A_i$, then it is possible to be accepted that K_i has achieved the required norm of reliability for the specific application of the software. However in the real programs it is impossible to test each sequence of operators because there may exist many thousands of operators. In this case if the sequence i is not tested then K_i can be extrapolated using the the the relation $K_i = E / M_t$, where M_t is the number of the tested sequences and E is the number of the errors found during the testing.

It can be considered, that the software modules work continuously, which is typical for the real time applications. In this case the distribution of the probability of failure of the software is two dimentional - one continuous for the time and another discrete for the input vectors, which is shown in Fig.6.3. While the probabilities P_i are not functions of the time, the probabilities K_i can decrease in the moments, when an error is found and properly corrected during the exploitation of the software. In Fig.6.3 this happens with K_5 in the moment t_2 .

2.3 A density function of the probability of failure

If it is considered that for each small unit of the time $\Delta t \approx dt$ the algorithm (Fig.6.1) is executed only ones , then the density function f(t) of the probability of failure $P_f(t)$ can be determined with the following equation:

$$\sum_{i=1}^{m} P_i K_i(t) \approx f(t) , \quad P_f(t) = \int_0^t f(t)\, dt \tag{6.5}$$

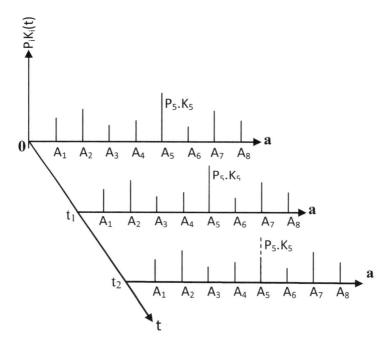

Fig. 6.3. A two dimensional distribution of the probability of failure

The value of $K_i(t)$ and the function $f(t)$ changes only in the moments when error is discovered during the normal working life of the software and is successfully corrected. In Fig.6.4 such moments are t_2 and t_3.

The density function of the probability of failure has the following properties:

a) $f(t)$ is a random function because the moments t_2, t_3 are random values.

b) The random function $f(t)$ has only one sample obtained during the life of the concrete software product.

c) The function $f(t)$ is unique and valid only for the concrete software.

d) As a density function of a probability, $f(t)$ must comply with the equation:

$$\int_0^{\infty} f(t)dt = 1 \qquad (6.6)$$

6.2.4 Function of the failure rate $\lambda(t)$ of the software module

In the reliability theory the failure rate function is widely used and for this reason should be determined also for the software. Usually it is considered that the distribution of $f(t)$ for electronic and computer systems is exponential, i.e. $f(t) = \lambda \cdot e^{-\lambda t}$. The real function $f(t)$ can be approximated with 3 different exponential distributions for the time intervals $t \in [0, t_2]$, $t \in [t_2, t_3]$, $t \in [t_3, \infty]$, accepting that for each interval λ is constant. The result in Fig.6.4 is that $\lambda_1 > \lambda_2 > \lambda_3$, but it is based on only one sample of the random function $f(t)$. The other researchers also can not have more exploitation samples for a given software product and therefore it is not wise to use sophisticated forms of $\lambda(t)$, as some researchers do [2,3].

6.3. Software safety model and on-line criterion for safety

In the recent years the analysis and management of software safety became one of the most important topics of the scientific research in the field of software [4,5,6,7]. Software failures f can be divided in two: dangerous f_d and non dangerous f_n: $f = f_d + f_n$, and accordingly the probabilities for failure are: $P_f = P_d + P_n$. The reliability of the software can be assessed by P_f and the safety - by P_d. This means that the main goal for improvement of the safety should be the reduction of the number of dangerous failures f_d and their reliability P_d. The specific measures for reduction of P_d include:
1. Hazard analysis and definition of the software modules, the failure of which can be dangerous.

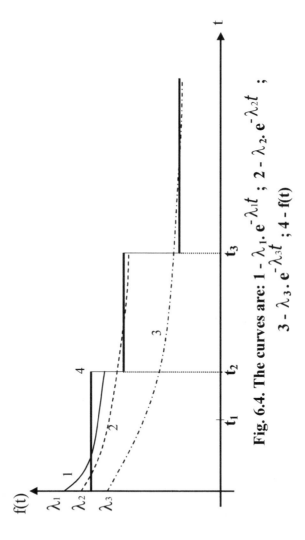

Fig. 6.4. The curves are: $1 - \lambda_1 \cdot e^{-\lambda_1 t}$; $2 - \lambda_2 \cdot e^{-\lambda_2 t}$; $3 - \lambda_3 \cdot e^{-\lambda_3 t}$; $4 - f(t)$

2. Application of the fault-tolerance strategy for the software dangerous modules or for the whole system, using different versions of software to perform the same task. When applied this strategy improves not only the software safety, but also the software reliability. According to many authors the application of the fault-tolerance strategy can't exclude all the errors in the software because the same sort of errors can be found in different versions of software, maid by different programmers, especially when their origin is in the specification of the software. That's why it is necessary to apply also the fail-safe strategy even when fault-tolerance strategy is used.

3.The fail-safe strategy is widely used in the hardware control systems but not in the software technology. It should be applied also in the software development. This strategy consist of two steps:

a) on-line detection of the failure of the software during the execution of the program, using a priori defined criterion for each module or for the whole system;

b) on-line transition of the controlled object to a safe state.

Concerning the step 3.a) the following criterion for safety can be suggested [9,10,14]:

Definition 1 : If the norm of the output $\| \mathbf{X}(t) \|$ does not belong to the allowable domain Ω of non dangerous output signals:

$$\| \mathbf{X}(t) \| \notin \Omega, \tag{6.7}$$

then can be considered that a dangerous failure of the software has occurred. This criterion can be applied on-line and can also be used as a basis for creation of a similar off-line criterion, which should be applied during the design and testing stage of the software.

In each specific case a proper norm $\| \mathbf{X}(t) \|$ should be sought. In the simplest cases the norms can be:

$$\sup_{0 \leq t \leq \infty} |x(t)| < \text{MAX} \quad \text{or} \qquad (6.8)$$

$$\inf_{0 \leq t \leq \infty} |x(t)| > \text{MIN} \ , \qquad (6.9)$$

where MAX and MIN are the allowable limits. Considering the on-line application of the criterion with the norm (6.8) the speed of the vehicle can be limited on-line and with the norm (6.9) the current of the excitation of D.C. motor should be stopped from dangerous falling. In another particular case Ω contains a set of allowable vectors of limited number of bits (i.e. codes) and $\mathbf{X}(t)$ can be compared with each element of Ω . In the general case however it is difficult to formulate a criterion for assessment of $\| \mathbf{X}(t) \|$, but in the most concrete cases it is possible. The assessment of the norms $\| \mathbf{X}(t) \|$ can be done by another processor or by the same processor if the problem of hardware reliability is solved.

Concerning the step 3.b) there are also in the general case theoretical and practical difficulties, but in the railway signaling systems this problem is solved - a red light appears in the semaphore and the train is stopped. What should be done in an aircraft or in a nuclear plant depends mainly on the concrete failure of the software and the system which is controlled . In some cases the condition (6.7), (6.8), (6.9) can be verified using hardware. For example for the limitation of the minimal current of excitation of a computer controlled drive with D.C. motors, a minimum current relay can be used.

6.4. Off-line application of the criterion of software safety

The described criterion (6.7) of software safety can be applied off-line during the design of the software, considering the software as a discrete nonlinear system with iterations:

$$\mathbf{X}_{n+1}(t+1) = F[\mathbf{X}(t), t, \mathbf{X}_n(t+1), P], \qquad (6.10)$$

$$X(0) \in Q_0, \quad t, t+1 \in [0,T],$$

where $X_{n+1}(t+1)$ and $X_n(t+1)$ are two consecutive iterations in the process of reaching the solution in the moment $(t+1)$, $X(t)$ is the vector solution in the moment t; the set Q_0 contains the initial values of the vector X, i.e. $X(0)$; P is a set of parameters used in the software and influencing the solution- $p=\{p_1, p_2,...p_j\}$, $p \in P$. The vector $X(t)$ describes the status of the system.. In the general case the right part of (6.10) is not an analytical function, but a system of procedures, subroutines and functions of the algorithmic language which is used.

In many cases Ω is simply connected domain Q, which can be defined in the following way:

$$Q\{ X : \|X\| \leq R_Q \}, \quad Q_0 \in Q, \tag{6.11}$$

where R_Q is the radius of the allowable domain. In this case the criterion (6.7) coincides with the following definition of practical stability of the software, suggested here on analogy with the definition of practical stability of analog systems [16].

Definition 2: For given sets (6.11) the discrete nonlinear system (6.10) modeling the software, with first iterations $X_0(1),...X_0(t+1) \in Q$, initial value $X(0) \in Q_0$ is practically stable for given Q_0, ε and time interval [0,T] if after (k+1) iterations

$$\|X_{k+1}(t+1) - X_k(t+1)\| < \varepsilon \tag{6.12}$$

and $X_{k+1}(t+1) \in Q$ for $(t+1) \in [0,T]$.

An additional explanation is that when after (k+1) iterations the condition (6.12) is satisfied, then $X_{k+1}(t+1)$ is approximating $X(t+1)$:

$$X(t+1) = X_{k+1}(t+1), \quad (t+1) \in [0,T]$$

Obviously the necessary number of iterations k+1 is different for each moment in the interval [0,T].The requirement $X_0(1),... X_0(t+1) \in Q$ means that the first iterations should belong to the set Q , which can be easily fulfilled. In Fig.6.5 a graphical explanation of *Definition 1* is given and practically stable process $X(0)...X(t+1)$ is shown.

The inequality (6.12) will be reached and the computational process will be convergent for a given t if the operator (6.10) written as $X_{n+1}= f [X_n]$ satisfies the Lipschitz condition:

$$\|f(x_1) - f(x_2)\| \le q \|x_1 - x_2\| \,, \qquad (6.13)$$

where q<1, and considering in this case x_1, x_2 as vectors.

The following criterion giving sufficient conditions for practical stability of software (and hence for software safety) in accordance with *Definition 2* is suggested in the following theorem [15]:

Theorem: The sufficient condition for practical stability of software described with equation (6.10) is:

$$\| X_{n+1}(t+1)\| = \|F[X(t), t, X_n(t+1), P]\| \le R_Q, \quad (6.14)$$

where the norm of the right part of (6.14) is evaluated taking into account that:

$$X(0) \in Q_0; \, t,t+1 \in [0,T], \, X(t) \in Q, \, X_n(t+1) \in Q, \, n \in [0,k+1]$$

Proof: It will be made using the method of mathematical induction. For this purpose it is necessary to be proven that:

1. The discrete process is stable in the initial moment ,i.e. $X(0) \in Q_0$ and each first iteration $X_0(1),...X_0(t+1) \in Q$.

2. If the system (6.10) is stable for the moment t, i.e. $X(t) \in Q$ and for iteration n in the moment t+1, i.e. $X_n(t+1) \in Q$ then the n+1 iteration in the moment t+1 is also stable and belongs to Q. However this second condition is fulfilled if the criterion (6.14) is satisfied. Then if using the induction method it follows that $X_{k+1}(t+1) \in Q$, which means that the theorem is proven according to *Definition 2* if the Lipschitz

condition (6.13) is satisfied.

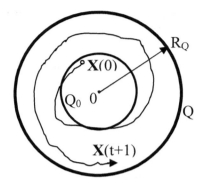

Fig. 6.5. Graphical explanation of *Definition 1*.

CONCLUSIONS

The main conclusions from the performed analysis and hazard identification of the software are:

1. The reliability and safety characteristics of the software are closely connected with the structure of the software and carried out verification test. It is not correct to use hypothetical reliability characteristics as many authors do.

2. For the safety critical systems both hazard analysis and criteria for software safety should be applied.

3. For the safety critical systems it is not enough to be applied only the fault-tolerant strategy, it is necessary to apply also the fail-safe strategy in the same system.

4. The hazard analysis and the off-line criteria for software safety are applied during the design stage of the systems.

5. The on-line criteria for software safety can be applied on-line during the functioning of the computer system for detection of dangerous failures not only in the algorithm and the program but also in hardware (in some cases).

6. The conclusions made above are valid in some extent for all computer controlled and computer designed systems.

REFERENCES

[1]. De Neumann, B. "Software certification", Elsevier applied science, 1988, UK.

[2]. Trachtenberg, M. A "General theory of software reliability modeling", IEEE Transaction on Reliability, vol. 39, No.1, April, 1990, pp.92-96.

[3]. SCHICK, G.J. and WOLVERTON, R.W. "An analysis of computing software reliability models", IEEE Transaction on software Engineering, vol. SE-4, Mar 1978, pp.104-120.

[4]. Hoare, T. "Maths adds safety to computer programs", Journal "New Scientist", 18 September, 1986, pp.53-56.

[5]. Redmill, F. "Technologies for software safety", Journal "Computing & Control", February, 1998, vol. 9, pp.2-3.

[6]. Redmill, F. "IEC-61508. Principles and use in the management of safety", Journal "Computing & Control", October 1998, vol.9, No.5, pp.205-213.

[7]. Parnas, D.L. and Van Schouwen, A.J. and Kwan, S.P. "Evaluation of safety critical software", Journal "Communication of the ACM", June 1990, vol.33, No. 6, pp.636-648.

[8]. Chudleigh, M. "Software and safety: how compatible are they?", Journal "Information and software technology", vol.32, No.5, June 1990, pp. 323-329.

[9]. Krumov, A. "One criterion for software safety", Proc. of the 8-th national scientific and applied science conference ELECRONICS'99, September 23-25, 1999, Sozopol, Bulgaria, pp. 91-95.

[10]. Krumov, A. "On the methodology of creation of ultrareliable and safe software" Proceedings of the International Scientific Conference "The transport of the 21st century" , Warszawa, Poland, September 19-21, 2001, Section IV , pp. 127-134.

[11]. Trzynadlowski, A.M. "Safe operating and safe design areas of induction motor drives" Industry Application Society Annual Meeting, 1994, Conference Record .

[12]. Lamden, R.J. "Project risk analysis in CAD", IEE Colloquium on Design Management Environments in CAD, Jan 1991, London, UK.

[13]. A. Krumov "A Structural Model of Software Reliability and Safety", Conference "Telematyca i Bezpieczenstwo Ruchu Dragowego"/in Polish/, October 25-26, 2002, Katowice, Poland.

[14] A. Krumov "Software reliability, safety and security", Proceedings of the third IEEE Workshop "Intelligent data acquisition and advanced computing systems"-IDAACS, Sofia, Bulgaria, Sept 5-7,2005, pp.429-434.

[15] A. Krumov "Hazard analysis and criteria for software safety in electrotechnics ", Proceedings of IEEE Conference MELECON 2006, Malaga, Spain, May 16-19, 2006, pp.843-846.

[16]. J. La Saal, S. Lefschetz , "Stability by Liapunov's direct method", Academic press, London, New York, 1961.

7 HAZARD ANALYSIS AND CRITERIA FOR SOFTWARE SAFETY IN ELECTRICAL SYSTEMS

7.1. Introduction

In the recent years the analysis and management of software safety became one of the most important topics of the scientific research in the field of software, but there are few papers concerning the specific problems of safety of computer aided engineering (CAE) software, consisting of computer aided design (CAD) [1], [2] and computer aided testing (CAT) software, especially in electrotechnics.

The first task when investigating the problem of software safety should be to carry out hazard analysis because all software should be regarded as safety critical until that is done [3], [4]. The safety analysis consists of three stages:

1. Hazard identification. This is important stage because the risks associated with unidentified hazard due to software errors can not be reduced.

2. Hazard analysis. The purpose of this analysis is to assess:
a) the probability of existence and manifestation of dangerous software errors during it exploitation;
b) the potential consequence of it.

3. Risk assessment. It employs the results of hazard analysis and can be quantitative or qualitative.

The mentioned above strategies have well known limitations and the probability of a dangerous failure in many cases can't be made acceptable. That's why some researchers try to find criteria for software safety [5].

In the present chapter an additional method [6] for improvement of software safety is suggested. It consists of synthesis of criteria of software safety which can be applied on-line and off-line. These criteria define the domains of non-dangerous output signals for each particular application. The off-line criterion, described in the previous chapter, can be used during the design of the software. The on-line criterion is applied during the functioning of the computer system and if a dangerous failure is detected a transition to a safe state of the controlled object is executed. The on-line criterion gives the sufficient conditions for dangerous failures of the computer system (not only software), while the off-line criterion gives the sufficient conditions for stability and safety.

The application of the mentioned above strategies is shown for some specific electrotechnical systems.

7.2. Hazard analysis of CAD software

For the purpose of this analysis a simplified flowchart is shown in Fig.7.1, describing the process of computer aided design-CAD in the general case. It consists of several blocks, which will be analyzed.

A. Block "Analytical calculations"

In this block for a given combination of the values of the parameters $\mathbf{X}=(x_1,x_2,...x_n)$, defining specific variant of the designed object (electrical motor, transformer or electrical device), the functional characteristics $\mathbf{F}=(f_1,f_2,...f_m)$ of the object are calculated:

$$\mathbf{F}=A(\mathbf{X}) \qquad (7.1)$$

The functional characteristics can concern the current and voltage stress of the different elements of the designed object, it's sizes, it's efficiency, torque, $\cos(\varphi)$, etc. and are specific for each object. In this block also are calculated and verified the constraints determining if the given variant is workable and non-dangerous:

$$\varphi_i(\mathbf{X},\mathbf{F}) \leq 0 , \quad i=1,2,...k \qquad (7.2)$$

For example φ_i can be:

$$f_i \leq s_i, \qquad (7.3)$$

where s_i is the allowed voltage or current value.

Analytically A and φ_i are represented with functions, functionals, operators (in the general case nonlinear) but their algorithmic and numerical forms consist of procedures, subroutines and functions (of the used programming language), usually working in a regime of iterations. Each variant of parameters **X**, satisfying the constraints (7.2) is considered workable without being optimal.

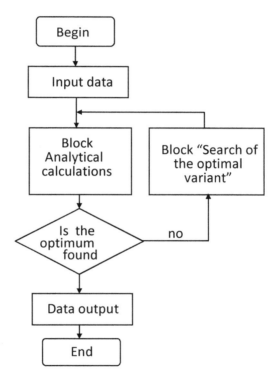

Fig.7.1. A simplified flowchart, describing the process of CAD.

Obviously an error in the block under consideration can lead to a wrong assessment of a variant as workable and non-dangerous when in reality the stresses or loads of some elements for example are bigger than the allowed values, which can have dangerous consequences.

B. Block "Search of the optimal variant"

All workable variants $\mathbf{X}_W$ of the designed object belong to the allowable domain Ω (Fig.7.2) of the parameters $\mathbf{X}$, defined by the constraints (7.2). However only one of the all workable variants - $\mathbf{X}_{opt}=(x_{1opt}, x_{2opt}, ... x_{nopt})$ is a global optimum for the accepted optimization criterion K:

$$K(\mathbf{X}_{opt}) = MIN_{global} \text{ or } MAX_{global} \tag{7.4}$$

Analytically the criterion K is a function, functional or operator, but its algorithmic and numerical realization uses iteratively procedures, functions, subroutines. It can assess for example the weight of electrical device for application in some vehicle or the price of electrical motor for general purpose application.

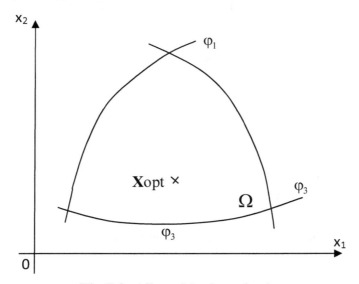

Fig.7.2. Allowable domain in two dimensional area.

60

The search of the optimal point $\mathbf{X}_{opt}$ in the domain Ω is the main goal of this block and different methods of search of the extremum - gradient, Monte-Carlo or scanning can be chosen and applied.

An error in this block can cause a wrong choice of the optimal variant, which can lead to bad economical results or other consequences. These consequences can not be dangerous because the wrongly chosen optimal variant will be checked for workability in the block of analytical calculations.

7.3. Hazard analysis of CAT software

For the purpose of this analysis a flowchart, concerning the general case of CAT (computer aided testing) software is suggested and shown in Fig.7.3. It consists of several blocks that will be analyzed.

A."Data acquisition" block

In this block the data, received from the transducers in the object under test, are read and written into the memory and after that- send to the monitor or printer.

An error in the software of this block can not lead to dangerous consequences, if the CAT system consists only of "Data acquisition " block without "Control block". However if there exist "Control block", then the erroneous data from the "Data acquisition" block will cause errors in the control signals with potentially dangerous consequences.

B. "Control block"

In this block control signals are calculated on the basis of the measured values obtained in the "Data acquisition" block. The erroneous calculation of the control signals in this block can have dangerous consequences if the objects under test have potentially dangerous characteristics - big power, high voltage, high speed, dangerous gases, radiation, etc.

When it is possible to define a domain Ω of the allowable values of the control signals then on-line and off-line criteria can be applied for verification whether the control signals belong to Ω. If this is not so, then transition to a safe state of the object under test should be performed. The on-line criterion protects from dangerous errors both in the "Data acquisition " block and in the algorithm or the program in the "Control block", while the off-line criterion is applied during the design stage of the "Control block" and protects from dangerous errors only in the algorithm and the program of this block.

In some extent the consideration made above is valid for all computer controlled systems.

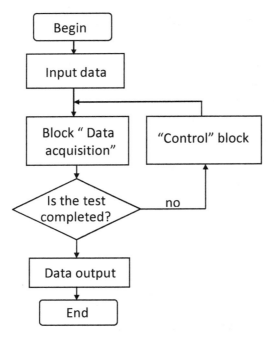

Fig.7.3. A simplified flowchart , describing the process of CAT.

CONCLUSIONS

1. An error in the block "Analitical calculations" of CAD can lead to a wrong assessment of a variant as workable and non-dangerous when in reality the stresses or loads of some elements are bigger than the allowed values, which can have dangerous consequences.

2. An error in the block "Search of the optimal variant"can cause a wrong choice of the optimal variant, which can lead to bad economical results, but these consequences usually can not be dangerous.

3. An error in the software of "Data acquisition " block can not lead to dangerous consequences, if the CAT system consists only of "Data acquisition " block without "Control block".

4. The erroneous calculation of the control signals in the "Control block", due to error in the input data or the algorithm and program can have dangerous consequences.

REFERENCES

[1] A.M. Trzynadlowski, "Safe operating and safe design areas of induction motor drives," *Industry Application Society Annual Meeting, 1994, Conference Record* .

[2] R.J. Lamden, "Project risk analysis in CAD," *IEE Colloquium on Design Management Environments in CAD,* Jan 1991, London, UK.

[3] P. Johannessen, C. Grante, A. Alminger, U. Eklund, J. Torin , "Hazard analysis in object oriented design of dependable systems," *Proceedings of the International Conference on Dependable Systems and Networks, 2001*, Gothenburg, Sweden

[4] B. De Neumann , *Software certification,* Elsevier applied science, 1988,UK.

[5] R.A. Gove, J.L.Heinzman , "Safety criteria and model for mission-critical embedded software systems", Computer Assurance, 1991. COMPASS '91, "Systems Integrity, Software safety and Process Security",

Proceedings of the Sixth Annual Conference on, 06/24/1991 - 06/27/1991 , Gaithersburg, MD USA, pp. 69 – 73.

[6] A. Krumov "Hazard analysis and criteria for software safety in electrotechnics", Proceedings of IEEE Conference MELECON 2006, Malaga, Spain, May 16-19, 2006, pp.843-846.

8 SAFETY CRITICAL COMPUTER SYSTEMS IN CARS

8.1. Preliminary Hazard Analysis (PHA)

Nowadays cars contain embedded systems that incorporate up to70 microcontrollers. A necessary first step in such a development process is the application of Preliminary Hazard Analysis (PHA). The purpose of PHA is the identification, classification and assessment of potential hazards of a newly developed vehicle that are caused by potential failures of its embedded system. The early application of PHA is required by the safety standard ISO26262 for automotive E/E system development.

The proposed methodology is explained in the following:

1. Definition of the Analysis Subject: First information concerning the vehicle under development is collected and modeled. Functions of the vehicle (e.g. motoring or recuperative braking) are described. In addition, requirements are associated with these functions.

2. Identification of Malfunctions and Hazards: Based on the definition of the analysis subject, possible malfunctions of the vehicle are identified.

3) Definition and Classification of Hazardous Events.

4) Derivation of Safety Goals: For each hazardous event that has a sufficiently high ASIL (Automotive Safety Integrity Level), a safety goal is defined and associated.

The contribution of the work [1] is a computer-aided approach to PHA in the development process of an automotive embedded system that is based on the domain-specific language EAST-ADL (Electronics Architecture and Software Technology-Architecture Description Language).

These properties can be automatically checked based on

the analysis model that reflects the results of the PHA. If properties are violated, the approach supports the automated identification of possible solutions and the automated correction of the analysis model. This guided and computer-aided approach strongly supports the application of PHA and the creation of an analysis model.

The proposed approach to PHA of automotive embedded systems was experimentally evaluated by the case study of HEV (Hybrid Electric Vehicles) development.

8.2. Fault Tree Analysis (FTA) and Failure Mode and Effect Analysis (FMEA)

In the paper [2] for the analysis of functional safety of Dual Clutch Transmission (DCT) control system, Fault Tree Analysis (FTA) and Failure Mode and Effect Analysis (FMEA) are applied. Functional safety is part of the overall safety and can be defined as: safety that the vehicle function does not cause any intolerable endangering state due to hazards caused by mal-functional behavior of E/E systems.

Once all the potential hazards have been identified in PHA (Preliminary Hazard Analysis) process, FMEA and FTA are used in system, sub-system and eventually, into component functional safety analysis. The chief difference between FMEA and FTA is a matter of depth. FMEA looks at all failures and their effects, while FTA is applied only to those effects that are potentially safety related and that are of the highest criticality.

FTA is an important and widely used safety analysis technique. It uses a logic diagram which starts with an undesirable top-level event and works downwards until the possible causes which lead to the top-level event have been identified. FTA uses Boolean logic (e.g. AND and OR gates) to depict the combinations of individual failure mode that can lead to the top-level event. A higher level event is the output of a gate, while the inputs to the gate are the lower level events. The faults can be events which are associated with component hardware failures, human errors, such as requirements errors, design errors and software bugs.

FMEA (Table 8.1) is widely used in the automotive industry, where they have served as a general purpose tool for enhancing reliability, trouble-shooting product and process issues, and as tool for functional safety analysis. FMEA analyses potential failure modes, effects, causes and determines a risk priority factor.

TABLE 8.1. SYSTEM-LEVEL FMEA

Item	Potential Failure Mode	Potential Effects of Failure	Potential Causes	RPN
	clutch1 disengaging failure clutch2 engaging failure	shifting failure; gear damage possible shifting failure loss of traction	dual-clutch mechatronic assembly fault dual-clutch mechatronic assembly fault	60
upshift process	shifting action failure	shifting failure loss of traction	shift mechatronic assembly fault	30

The paper [3] deals with the partial automation of cars for safety purposes. The main aim of this paper is to develop a low cost, partially automated system that can be installed in a manually driven car for the prevention of collision, which does not take away the pleasure of driving. The paper essentially consists of three parts: a) the sensor system; b) the processing system; c) the mechanical systems of the car.

The proposed system consists of the basic blocks like transducers, microcontrollers, multiplexers and the braking, steering, acceleration systems of the car. The basic electronic system and the control algorithms are also shown in the paper. Features like alerting the driver with the collision on all four sides with the help of a LCD display can be easily achieved.

The contribution of the work [4] is twofold: First, methods for improving requirement specification based on natural languages are presented. Second, methods for the efficient analysis of the ISO26262 process are provided.

According to standards (like CMMI, Automotive SPICE, ISO26262) requirements are hierarchically grouped to:

(1) system requirements;

(2) software/hardware requirements;

(3) software/hardware component requirements.

8.3. ISO26262 and ASIL

One of the core concepts of ISO26262 is the so called AUTOMOTIVE SAFETY INTEGRITY LEVEL, short ASIL. The ASIL decomposition allows the separation of products into safety relevant parts, and is a result of the following activities:

•Hazard and risk analysis ("What could happen if...")

• Preparation of a safety concept (e.g. "What is the safe state")

• Elicitation of safety requirements (e.g. "How to provide the safe state")

• SIL decomposition (e.g. "What SIL applies for individual units").

In paper [5], a comprehensive software hazard analysis method is presented, which applies a number of hazard analysis techniques such as Preliminary Hazard Analysis (PHA), Fault Tree Analysis (FTA) and Failure Mode and Effect Analysis (FMEA) (Table 8.2) for Automated Manual Transmission (AMT) control system.

Software Functions		Potential Failure Mode Due to Software	Potential Effects of Failure	Potential Severity	RPN
Upshift Module	Clutch Disengaging/ Engaging	Failure in Acquiring Sensor Signal Failure;	No Senor Signals Can be Read; Some or All Sensor Signals Incorrect	10	60
		Failure in Calculating Command Failure;	Incorrect Control Command; Incorrect Timing Erroneous Returning Address	10	60
		Failure in Delivery of Command to Actuator	Incorrect Control Command; No Control Command	10	60
	Shifting Action	Failure in Acquiring Sensor Signal Failure;	No Senor Signals Can be Read; Some or All Sensor Signals Incorrect	10	80
		Failure in Calculating Command Failure;	Incorrect Control Command; Incorrect Timing Erroneous Returning Address	10	80
		Failure in Delivery of Command to Actuator	Incorrect Control Command; No Control Command	10	80

Table 8.2 System-Level Software FMEA

The basic steps for performing a PHA are:

1. Perform brainstorming to identify potential hazards associated with the system.
2. Provide a description of the hazard, and potential accidents associated with the hazard.
3. Identify potential causes of the hazard.
4. Determine the risk of the hazard and accidents.
5. Determine whether controls can be added to the system to eliminate or mitigate the risks.

A key component of this methodology is an integrated PHA, FTA and FMEA for investigating potential software causes of system hazards. The combinations of these techniques can lead to a more thorough analysis result, since each considers the analysis problem from a different point of view. Table 8.2 is an example of FMAE.

REFERENCES

[1]. Roland Mader, Gerhard Grießnig, Andrea Leitner, Christian Kreiner, Quentin Bourrouilh1, Eric Armengaud, Christian Steger, Reinhold Weiß "A Computer-Aided Approach to Preliminary Hazard Analysis for Automotive Embedded Systems", 2011, 18th IEEE International Conference and Workshops on Engineering of Computer-Based Systems.

[2]. Hongkun Zhang, Wenjun Li, and Jun Qin "Model-based Functional Safety Analysis Method for Automotive Embedded System Application", International Conference on Intelligent Control and Information Processing, August13-15, 2010-Dalian, China.

[3]. Abhinav Ray, Varun Kumar "Safety-Automation of Cars Using Embedded Microcontrollers", Proceedings of the 2005 International Conference on Computational Intelligence for Modelling, Control and Automation, and International Conference on Intelligent Agents, Web Technologies and Internet

Commerce (CIMCA-IAWTIC'05).

[4]. Martin Krammer, Nadja Marko, Eric Armengaud, Gerhard Griessnig "Improving Methods and Processes for the Development of Safety Critical Automotive Embedded Systems", 978-1-4244-6850-8/10/$26.00 ©2010 IEEE.

[5]. Wenjun Li, Hongkun Zhang "A Software Hazard Analysis Method for Automotive Control System", 978-1-4244-8728-8/11/$26.00 ©2011 IEEE .

9 INTRUSION-TOLERANT SYSTEMS

9.1. Definition

Quite often failures in network based services and server systems may not be accidental or caused by incorrectness of a program, but rather caused by deliberate security intrusions. So software security can be achieved by software, which continues to function correctly under malicious attacks. Internet-enabled software applications present the most common security risk encountered today.

9.2. Measures for achievement of the necessary level of software security

Most organizations manage computer security risk reactively by investing in technologies designed to protect against known system vulnerabilities and monitor intrusions as they occur [1]. However, firewalls, cryptography, and antivirus protection address the symptoms, not the root cause, of most security problems. It is important to treat security as an decisive attribute and develop an intrusion tolerant system and compute the "mean time to security failure – $m=1/\lambda$ " and the probabilities of security failure.

Buying and maintaining a firewall, for example, is ineffective if external users can access remotely exploitable Internet-enabled applications through it. Because hackers attack software, improving computer security depends on proactively managing risks associated with software and software development. The current approach of fixing broken software only after it has been compromised is insufficient to control the problem .

Network based services and server systems should either completely preclude the possibility of a security intrusion or design them to be robust enough to continue functioning despite security attacks. Not only is it important to prevent security intrusions, it is equally important to treat security as an decisive attribute and develop an **intrusion tolerant system**. A security intrusion and the response of an intrusion tolerant system to the attack is modeled in [2] as a random process. This facilitates the use of stochastic modeling techniques to capture the attacker behavior as well as the system's response to a security intrusion. This model is used to compute the "mean time to security failure" and also compute probabilities of security failure due to violations of different security attributes.

Given the high cost of producing software, development of technology for prevention of software piracy is important for the software industry. In [3] a novel approach for preventing the creation of unauthorized copies of software is presented. The software modules are split into open and hidden components. The open components are installed on an insecure machine while the hidden components are installed on a secure machine. It is assumed that while open components can be stolen, to obtain a fully functioning copy of the software, the hidden components must be recovered.

Many security processes can be embedded into software's development to make it more secure. Some examples from Microsoft's Secure Development Life Cycle (SDLC; www.microsoft.com/security/sdl/default.aspx) include security requirements, threat modeling, static analysis, dynamic analysis, security review, and product incident response. Each security process has its strengths and weaknesses. Measure of a process's values are:
a) the quantity of important security defects it can detect;
b) another is how early in the development process it can be performed (thus making correction less expensive);
c) third measure is how automated the process can be (automation reduces the cost of applying the process).

Static analysis [11] fares well by all of these measures, which has helped it to become one of the most popular security tools used during software development. Static analysis should occur early in software development to reduce vulnerabilities.

Advances in hard disk technologies can help manage the complexity of operating system security and enforce security policies.

The Switch Blade architecture provides isolation for multiple OSs running on a machine by confining them into segments that users can only access using a physical token. This solution gives a way of protecting the OS by forming a trusted path directly between the storage and the user. It is realized, that many users are running more than one OS from the same disk.

Email is especially dangerous because nearly all organizations allow email to enter their networks. In mid-2005, the UK National Infrastructure Security Co-ordination Centre1 and the US Computer Emergency Response Team2 issued technical alert bulletins about targeted emails that drop Trojans to exfiltrate sensitive information. The intrusions evaded conventional firewall and antivirus capabilities, and enabled adversaries to harvest sensitive information. In 2007, various government agencies experienced intrusion attempts.

9.3. Testing

Done properly, testing software security [4] goes deeper than simple **black-box** probing on the presentation layer (performed by so-called application security tools) - and even beyond the functional testing of security apparatus.

Testing for software security [5] is a lengthy, complex and costly process. Currently security testing is done using penetration analysis and formal verification of security kernels. These methods are not complete and are difficult to use. Hence it is essential to focus testing effort in areas that have a greater number of security vulnerabilities to develop secure software as well as meet budget and time constraints. A testing strategy is proposed, based on a classification of vulnerabilities to develop secure and stable systems. This enables the system testing and maintenance group to understand the distribution of security vulnerabilities and prioritize their testing effort according to the impact the vulnerabilities have on the system. This is based on Landwehr's (1994) classification scheme for security flaws and evaluated it using a database of operating system vulnerabilities. This analysis indicates vulnerabilities tend to be focused in relatively few areas and associated with a small number of software engineering issues.

The paper [6] describes a security assessment instrument for the software development and maintenance life cycle. The assessment instrument is a collection of tools and procedures to support development of secure software. Specifically, the instrument offers a formal approach for engineering network security into software systems and application throughout the software development and maintenance life cycle. The instrument also includes a set of Security Assessment Tools (SAT), including the development of a property-based testing tool, to slice software code looking for specific vulnerability properties. Another component of the research is an investigation into the verification of software designs for compliance to security properties. This is based on innovative model checking approaches that will facilitate the development and verification of software security models.

A software security tester can properly focus on areas

of code in which an attack is likely to succeed by identifying risks in the system and creating tests driven by those risks. This approach provides a higher level of software security assurance than is possible with classical **black-box** testing, which is testing software based on output requirements and without any knowledge of the internal structure or coding in the program. The term is also used to test a Web site's vulnerability without having any knowledge of the Web server infrastructure. Read more in:

http://www.answers.com/topic/black-box-testing#ixzz2G5OyMQZ3

It is essential to focus testing effort in areas that have a greater number of security vulnerabilities to develop secure software as well as meet budget and time constraints. The testing strategy should be based on a classification of vulnerabilities to develop secure and stable systems and verification of software. Secure software development techniques should use threat modeling or **white box testing** for development of Attack-Resistant Software, which is testing of the software with the knowledge of the internal structure and coding inside the program. The term is also used to test a Web site's vulnerability after obtaining network data such as IP addresses and network diagrams. Read more in:

http://www.answers.com/topic/white-box-testing-technology#ixzz2G5ODflAC

9.4. Information assurance

Many authors have regarded software assessment as a way to determine the correctness of software. For this purpose formal methods and testing are used. However the correct and safe behaviors may not coincide since **safety is a system property while correctness is a software property**. Information assurance is similar to software assurance but covers a broader set of information integrity issues, such as **information security, privacy, and**

confidentiality [7]. For example, if a system can withstand attacks, whether malicious or simply unfortunate, and still provide accurate information on demand, then it provides some degree of information assurance. **Information assurance also includes software safety, software security, reliability, fault tolerance, correctness, and so on**. Information assurance exist if accurate enough information is available on demand for a given application or situation.

REFERENCES

[1] G. McGraw, "Managing software security risks," Computer, April 2002, Volume: 35, Issue:4, page(s):99 – 101.

[2] B. B. Madan, K. Gogeva-Popstojanova, K. Vaidyanathan, K.S Trivedi, "Modeling and quantification of security attributes of software systems", Dependable Systems and Networks, 2002. Proceedings- International Conference on, Publication Date: 23-26 June 2002, page(s): 505 – 514.

[3] Xiangyu Zhang, R. Gupta, " Hiding program slices for software security," Code Generation and Optimization, 2003, CGO 2003. International Symposium on, Publication Date: 23-26 March 2003, page(s): 325 – 336.

[4] B. Potter, G. McGraw, "Software security testing," Security & Privacy Magazine, IEEE, Volume 2, Issue 5, Sept.-Oct. 2004, Page(s):81 – 85.

[5] K. Jiwnani, M. Zelkowitz , " Maintaining software with a security perspective," Software Maintenance, 2002, Proceedings, International Conference on 3-6 Oct. 2002 , page(s): 194 – 203.

[6] D. P. Gilliam, J. C. Kelly, J. D. Powell, M. Bishop, "Development of a software security assessment instrument to reduce software security risk," "Enabling Technologies: Infrastructure for Collaborative

Enterprises", 2001, WET ICE 2001, Proceedings- Tenth IEEE International Workshops on, 20-22 June 2001, page(s):144 – 149.

[7] J. Voas, "Protecting against what? The Achilles heel of information assurance," Software, IEEE, Jan.-Feb. 1999, 16, Issue: 1, page(s): 28 – 29.

[8] Michael Malkin, Thomas Wu, Dan Boneh "Building intrusion-tolerant applications", Project URL: http://www.stanford.edu/~dabo/ITTC.

[9] Toshikazu Uemura, Tadashi Dohi, NaotoKaio "Availability Analysis of an Intrusion Tolerant Distributed Server System With Preventive Maintenance", IEEE Transactions on Reliability, vol.59, No.1, March 2010.

[10] Kevin Butler, Stephen Mclaughlin, Thomas Moyer, Patrick Mcdaniel "New Security Architectures Based on Emerging Disk Functionality", 1540-7993/10/$26.00 © 2010 IEEE, September/October 2010, copublished by the IEEE Computer and Reliability Societies.

[11] Paul E. Black "Static Analyzers: Seat Belts for Your Code", IEEE Security & Privacy, May/June 2012.

10 HAZARD ANALYSIS AND SAFETY OF EMBEDDED SYSTEMS

The term "Safety-Critical Systems" is used to describe those systems or applications in which failure can lead to serious injury, loss of life, significant property damage, or damage to the environment.

Safety and reliability requirements of a safety-critical system differ on the type of failure, whether it is a safe or an unsafe failure. Therefore, the use of a fault-tolerance method is not enough to guarantee that the required system will be safe.

In order to cover the safety management of safety critical systems through out their life cycles, many safety standards have been proposed like: MIL-STD-882D which is a military standard, and IEC61508 which is application-independent standard. These standards use the level of residual risk in the required system as a metric for safety. They provide definitions of risk both in terms of severity and probability.

In the paper [1] four methods: NVP, RB, AV and RBBV were simulated with different values of probability of failure:

a) **N-Version Programming (NVP)** runs the diverse versions in parallel on N hardware modules and uses a voting technique to perform a fault masking.

b) **Recovery Block.** In RB, the independent versions are executed sequentially followed by an acceptance test (AT) on a single hardware component. After the execution of the first version, the acceptance test is executed to check if the outcome is reasonable and to detect any possible erroneous result. If the acceptance test is passed, then the outcome is considered as true. Otherwise, if a fault is detected, the system state should be restored to its original state and an alternate version will be invoked to repeat the same computations. This process is repeated until either one of the alternate versions passes the test and gives the result, or no more versions are available. In the last case, an overall system failure is reported to execute the available safety function.

c) **Acceptance Voting (AV).** AV pattern incorporates the NVP with the acceptance test used in the RB. This pattern executes the diverse versions in parallel on N hardware modules. The output of each version is verified for correctness using an acceptance test and only those results that pass the acceptance test are used by the voting algorithm to generate the final result. The goal of the AV is to mask the faulty outputs from participating in the voting process.

d) **Recovery Block with Back up Voting (RBBV).** RBBV is an extension to the classical RB pattern, improves the reliability of the classical RB in those situations where it is difficult to construct an efficient acceptance test. It solves the problem of false negative cases which include a wrongly consideration of the correct output by the AT as erroneous output.

In [3] FPGAs (Field Programmable Logic Arrays) and MCUs (Microcontrollers) are compared, with respect on their **suitability for safety-critical applications**. In principle, a certain functionality could be realized on both types of hardware platforms (MCU or FPGA based). Depending on the functional and non-functional requirements, one hardware platform might be suited better than another one. Based on the results of the experiments, no general advantages in verification of real-time behavior could be found for FPGAs or MCUs. As another result, FPGAs allow a good separation of real-time functions, while this separation is more complicated on MCUs (functions are usually coupled by a single CPU on MCUs). These experiments in [3] are focused on software faults only, but in safety-critical applications hardware faults have to be taken into consideration too.

According to [2] software systems are developed following various safety standards - IEC61508, ISO26262, ISO14971. One common method used for this purpose is "Fault Tree Analysis" ("FTA"). FTA is a deductive top-down method that is used to derive the failure mode, called a top event, in terms of logical combinations of basic events, i.e., events or conditions that cannot be decomposed further in a way that is useful for the analysis. In Fig.10.1 the top event (the failure of Subsystem A) can be result of the failures of the basic events (1 AND 2) OR 6 OR (3 AND 4 AND 5) OR (7 AND 8). The failure can be for example erroneous logical "1".

In the paper [2] the authors describe an approach to use the results of FTA for the construction of test models - test cases can be derived, selected and prioritized according to the severity of the identified risks and the number of basic events that cause it. This approach is demonstrated on an example from the automation domain, namely a modular production system. It was found that the method provides a significant increase in coverage of safety functions, compared to regular model-based testing. By risk-based testing, test case derivation is controlled using risk information given in fault trees, so that possible failure modes are tested in order of criticality, where criticality is a measure derived from fault probability (as given by the number of basic events) and severity that describes the expected damage caused by the occurrence of a failure mode over a given time frame.

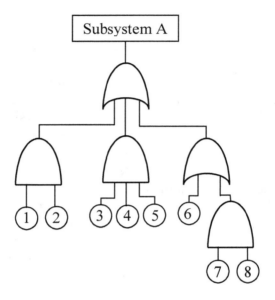

Figure 10.1. FTA diagram.

The embedded use of Programmable Electronic Systems (PESs) in safety-critical applications has been analyzed in [4]. The RTOS (Real-Time Operating System) of the proposed PES, based on the task concept of the Process and Experiment Automation Real time Language (PEARL), which was standardized as DIN66253-2(1998). One of this language's interesting features is the direct notion of time. This enables exact and problem-oriented specification of timing conditions to activate, terminate, suspend, continue, or resume tasks.

The standard IEC61508 recommends various techniques to reduce the influence of hardware failures. However applying these measures would significantly increase complexity and infringe the strategy of design for simplicity. As a remedy, a redundant configuration of PESs is employed connecting all system nodes, via rings and transferring data from node to node as in a shift register.

In [7] the author analyzes the software errors in the spacecrafts Voyager, which has 18000 lines of source code and Galileo with 22000 lines of source code. The conclusion is that the reasons for safety-related software errors are:

1). Discrepancies between the documented requirement specifications and the requirements needed for correct functioning of the system;

2). Misunderstanding of the software interfaces with the rest of the system.

In [8] several basic methods are discussed:

Concerning the formal methods, one possible approach to qualifying embedded software, uses formal verification techniques such as model checking and theorem proving. Yet no one has ever formally verified a multimillion-line safety-critical system in its entirety.

During the 1980s and early 1990s France introduced three different languages designed for model-driven synthesis of embedded control software:

Esterel (www.esterel-technologies.com),

SIGNAL: (www.irisa.fr/espresso/Polychrony),

and Lustre:

(www-verimag.imag.fr/~synchron/index.php?page=lang-design).

Lustre and SIGNAL provide data-flow description languages that are closest to the mathematical-equation expression of the control-problem solution.

While the approach of MATLAB/Simulink: (www.mathworks.com/products/simulink),

Labview (www.ni.com/labview),
and Ptolemy (www.ptolemy.eecs.berkeley.edu)
is model-based, it does not guarantee correctness through constructively correct synthesis.

The SCADE tool—commercialized by Esterel technologies and based on the Lustre language, is still used widely in AirBus flight-control software generation. Further, SCADE is but one of several languages for model-driven engineering in Europe.

In [9] the safety and security requirements are integrated with the rest of the systems requirements in the form of integrated behavior tree. The method is implemented in medical ambulatory infusion pump. For the purpose of security the reset of the pump functions is possible only after entering the correct password.

REFERENCES

[1]. Ashraf Armoush, Eva Beckschulze, Stefan Kowalewski "Safety Assessment of Design Patterns for Safety-Critical Embedded Systems", 35th Euromicro Conference on Software Engineering and Advanced Applications, 2009.

[2]. Johannes Kloos, Tanvir Hussain, Robert Eschbach "Risk-based Testing of Safety-Critical Embedded Systems Driven by Fault Tree Analysis", Fourth International Conference on Software Testing, Verification and Validation Workshops, 2011.

[3]. Falk Salewski, Stefan Kowalewski "The Effect of Hardware Platform Selection on Safety-Critical Software in Embedded Systems: Empirical Evaluations", 1-4244-0840-7/07/$20.00 02007 IEEE.

[4]. Martin Skambraks, Wolfgang A. Halang "Architectural Concepts for Embedded Systems in Safety-critical Applications", 1-4244-2577-8/08/$20.00 © 2008 IEEE.

[5]. I. Bate, A. Burns "A Framework For Scheduling In Safety Critical Embedded Control Systems", 0-7695-

0306-3/99 $10.00 1999 IEEE.

[6]. Zhidong Qin, Hui Chen, Youqun Shi "Reliability Demonstration Testing Method for Safety-Critical Embedded Applications Software", The 2008 International Conference on Embedded Software and Systems (ICESS2008).

[7]. Robyn R. Lutz "Analyzing Software Requirements Errors In Safety-Critical Embedded Systems", 0-8186-3120-1/92 $3.00 1992 IEEE.

[8]. Sandeep K. Shukla, "Model-Driven Engineering and Safety-Critical Embedded Software", 0018-9162/09/$26.00 © 2009, IEEE Computer Society, September, 2009.

[9]. Saad Zafar, R. G. Dromey "Integrating Safety and Security Requirements into Design of an Embedded System", Proceedings of the 12th Asia-Pacific Software Engineering Conference (APSEC'05), 0-7695-2465-6/05$20.00©2005, IEEE.

11 DEPENDABILITY OF EMBEDDED SYSTEMS

Safety-critical embedded systems need to be dependable. The notion of dependability is broken down into six fundamental properties [1], as was shown in chapter 2:
(1) reliability;
(2) availability;
(3) safety;
(4) confidentiality;
(5) integrity;
(6) maintainability.

The first step in developing a dependable embedded system is to define the dependability requirements.

The next step is to determine the system hazards. Hazards are system states that could lead to undesirable outcomes which result from using a system. Hazards are not obvious, and determining the hazards for a given system is often a difficult and complex task.

There are two basic types of fault: **degradation faults** and **design faults**. Degradation faults arise over time, and a component that operates correctly for some period of time might stop doing so as a result of a degradation fault. Degradation faults have to be expected, and, if such faults could lead to failure, the system has to be designed to operate acceptably after such faults have occurred. This concept is referred to as fault tolerance. Thus fault tolerance is a mechanism by which, dependability property (such as availability) is achieved. A design fault is something that is wrong with a system that has been there from the beginning. It is not the result of a component wearing out. **All software faults are design faults** because software does not degenerate in the usual sense.

In a fault-tolerant system, it is usually the case that

software implements the fault tolerance designed to deal with hardware faults. The software must be written in such way to diagnose the situation, and switch to a simple but safe emergency algorithm.

The Achilles' heel of software development for embedded systems is requirements specification. Verification is another major challenge in the development of software for embedded applications. Running tests on an embedded system is difficult because test hardware have to duplicate a complex embedded environment.

In paper [2] the dependability assessment of three cores, a PIC and an 8051 microcontroller, representative of microcontrollers commonly used in embedded applications were investigated, applying fault emulation. They present a Reduced and Complex Instruction Set Computer architecture, respectively. The third core is a custom design of a specific-purpose DSP-like architecture. The results are shown for different types of faults. For example **Mean-Time-To-Failure (MTTF)** is: DSP = $1/1105\lambda$, PIC=$1/721\lambda$, 8051=$1/641\lambda$, where λ is the standard failure rate $\lambda=10^{-11}$ faults/hour for flip-flops (FFs). According to the experimental emulation data 8051 core presents the lowest failure rate (22.98%) and thus it could be a suitable candidate for its integration in a highly available system. However, when dealing with the system's safety, the PIC core presents the lowest probability of reaching an unsafe state (71.9%).

Another problem during operation is that electrical properties of chips change over time, a phenomenon known as aging effects. Various stress situations like thermal cycling trigger these effects. Such stress situations might cause the circuits to fail after a certain period of operation or to degrade or change its initial electrical and physical properties.

In [3] authentication within the X86 CPU system management mode has significant benefits for system security. Applications can use the BIOS interface to get system security-sensitive information. This is safe for systems as long as we can check applications and block unauthorized ones that are attempting to obtain security data. To address these issues, a BIOS security-related service and interface-protection mechanism was developed. The basic idea is that only an approved software application or an individual with knowledge of the cipher can use the kernel BIOS service, which is very sensitive to system configuration and stability. If malicious software wants to crack this mechanism, it must obtain the key for decrypting the application code. Because the decrypt key is loaded into System Manager RAM, however, it's in a safe location, where it's invisible to the rest of the system.

In [4] the authors define embedded markets affected by software assurance issues, then examine ways in which security and assurance capabilities are partitioned in hardware and software. They then look at the problems inherent to configuring secure hardware. Three distinct assurance issues exist across several embedded computing markets (see Table 11.1).

One advantage of embedded security in hardware is its ability to guarantee device and hardware uniqueness through various technologies that can be selectably readable. The key capabilities let embedded developers to make encryption with the hardware identification code.

Software is widely considered the system element most vulnerable to malware. Dividing application tasks into separate operating cores (multi-core hardware) or virtual machines (software) offer a new toolset for security engineers to trade flexibility and security.

Table 11.1. Embedded markets with security and other assurance requirements.

Embedded markets	Code-base assurance	Safety assurance	Transaction assurance
Automotive	Proprietary design	Safety-critical	
Handheld	Proprietary design		Financial transaction
Military/ aerospace	Classified systems	Safety-critical	
Data storage	Proprietary design		Personal data

The two primary government standards for providing end-system assessment of combined hardware/embedded software security are: FIPS directives from the US National Institute of Standards and Technology (NIST) and the Common Criteria Evaluation Assessment Level Accreditations from NIAP (US National Information Assurance Partnership): (www.commoncriteriaportal.org).

Several authors use the terms "Embedded systems" and **"Cyber-Physical Systems"** as synonyms [5].

Also according to Wikipedia:
(http://en.wikipedia.org/wiki/Cyber-physical_system),

"a cyber-physical system (CPS) is a system featuring a tight combination of, and coordination between, the system's computational and physical elements."

"Today, we find a generation of cyber-physical systems in areas as diverse as aerospace, automotive, chemical processes, civil infrastructure, energy, healthcare, manufacturing, transportation, entertainment, and consumer appliances. This generation is often referred to as embedded systems".

In paper [6] four topics are discussed:

I. Dependability Issues due to Technology Effects and Architectural Countermeasures. Undependability addressed within this part is related to: a) Fabrication and Design-Time Effects like "Process Variations"; b) Run-time effects as "Aging Effects", "Thermal Effects".

II. Reliability Aware Design for Embedded Systems.

New architectural features are required for robust system design with built-in mechanisms for failure tolerance, detection and recovery during normal system operation. This part of the paper will focus on new design techniques required for building robust systems: concurrent error detection, recovery, and self-repair.

III. Security Attacks in Embedded Systems.

Typical security attacks are: physical, logical/software-based and side-channel/lateral attacks. **Physical attacks** refer to unauthorized physical access to the embedded system itself and are feasible only when the attacker has direct access to the system. **Logical attacks** exploit weaknesses in logical systems such as software or a cryptographic protocol to gain access to unauthorized information. **Side-channel attacks** are performed by observing properties of the system (such as power consumption, electromagnetic emission, etc.) while the system performs cryptographic operations.

IV. Countermeasures Against Security Attacks.

They could broadly be categorized into software based techniques and hardware assisted techniques. **Software based techniques** use software tools such as code analyzers and methods such as proof-carrying-code to overcome these attacks without changing the architecture of the processor. **Hardware assisted techniques** use additional hardware blocks or microarchitectural support to detect and protect against these security attacks.

Numerous real time and embedded control systems are safety related. Hence, the software involved must be rigorously verified, i.e., safety licensed, since it is far from being as dependable as hardware. Licensing, however, is very critical and difficult, and satisfactory methods are still missing. In this connection in paper [7] the following measures and questions are suggested:

1). Safety Related Real Time Software. These so-called "embedded computer systems" pervade all areas of our lives, allowing for higher productivity and flexible adaptation. They have the special property that hardware and software are closely coupled to form complex mixed-technology systems.

Hardware is subject to wear, transient faults, and unintended environmental influences. **Software, on the other hand, does not wear out,** nor can environmental circumstances cause software faults. Instead, software is imperfect with all errors, being design errors, i.e., of systematic nature, and their causes always being latently present. Software defect density is more or less unchanged in the last 20 years.

2) Formal methods. According to Advanced Study Institute (NATO) on Real Time Computing, while formal descriptions are valuable, the state-of-the-art has not evolved to a point, yet, where they can be widely applied. Application of formal verification techniques requires special mathematical expertise. The lengthy program correctness proofs inevitably lead to human errors which may remain undetected by peer review and may persist for long times. Therefore, formal methods turn out to be inappropriate for rigorous software verification as well, because they do not pay tribute to the human element.

3) Safety by Simplicity. It can be achieved with approaches centered around simplicity as the appropriate fundamental design principle of Dijkstra: "So we better learn how not to introduce complexity in the first place. The moral is clear: prevention is better than cure, in particular if the illness is unmastered complexity, for which no cure exists".

4). Construction of Safe Software. To prove that a larger program fulfills the requirements of a safety related automation system, currently only the technique of diverse **back translation** is available. Thus, to circumvent the problem of non-safety-licensed compilers, correctness proofs must be based on considering object code, i.e., the only form of programs available to machines executing them. It takes care of the fact that safety licensing of programs cannot be based on high level language representations, as there is no compiler, yet, whose correct operation has been verified.

REFERENCES

[1]. John C. Knight "Dependability of Embedded Systems", ZCSE'02, May 19-25, 2002, Orlando, Florida, USA.

[2]. David de Andrés, Juan-Carlos Ruiz, Daniel Gil, Pedro Gil "Dependability Assessment for the Selection of Embedded Cores", Seventh European Dependable Computing Conference, 978-0-7695-3138-0/08 $25.00 © 2008 IEEE DOI 10.1109/EDCC-7.2008.19.

[3]. Hui Jun (Kevin) Wu "Kernel Service Protection for Client Security", Copublished by the IEEE Computer and Reliability societies, 1540-7993/10/$26.00 © 2010

IEEE, September/October 2010.

[4]. J. Ryan Kenny, Craig Robinson, "Embedded Software Assurance for Configuring Secure Hardware", Copublished by the IEEE Computer and Reliability societies, 1540-7993/10/$26.00 © 2010 IEEE, September/October 2010.

[5]. Ram Chillarege, Jeffrey Voas "Reliability of Embedded and Cyber-Physical Systems", Copublished by the IEEE Computer and Reliability societies, 1540-7993/10/$26.00 © 2010 IEEE, September/October 2010.

[6]. Jörg Henkel, Vijaykrishnan Narayanan, Sri Parameswaran, Roshan Ragel "Security and Dependability of Embedded Systems: A Computer Architects' Perspective", 2009, 22nd International Conference on VLSI Design, DOI 10.1109/VLSI.Design.2009.114.

[7]. Wolfgang A. Halang "Software Dependability Considered as the Main Problem of Embedded Systems", ICIT 2003 - Maribor, Slovenia, 0-7803-7852-0/03/$17.00 02003 IEEE.

12 METHOD AND ALGORITHM FOR ACCELERATED RELIABILITY TESTING

With increasing quality requirements of computer systems and electronic and electrical components from which they are made, is increasing the interest in their reliability- the most important characteristic of quality. In most cases, however, it is difficult to investigate in reasonable time reliability of a device or of parts from it. That's why accelerated tests are applied. They are carried out under aggravated conditions and the obtained in short time reliability data of the devices are used for assessment /by mathematical calculations – approximation and extrapolations/ of reliability under normal operating conditions.

The purpose of this chapter is to suggest method and algorithm (for creation of computer program), which can be used for accelerated reliability tests of electrical, electronic and computer devices and parts.

12.1. Theoretical background

In the reliability testing there is connection between the time of reliable operation, without failure τ, the environmental factor t and the criterion U.

$$\tau = f(t,U) \tag{12.1}$$

For electrical and electronic products environmental factor is usually the ambient temperature t and the breakdown voltage is often assumed as criterion, if the insulation is tested [1]. In other cases the criterion U is the level of vibration [7] or moisture environments [5].

In the general case an approximation:

$$\tau = f_1(t).f_2(U) \tag{12.2}$$

of (12.1) can be sought. For the electrical and electron devices it is known that there is exponential relation between τ, t and U:

$$\tau = e^{at+\,bU+\,c} = \exp(at + bU + c) \qquad (12.3)$$

On the bases of the data obtained during the accelarated tests, the optimal values of the constants a, b, c should be calculated, applying the developed for this purpose algorithm. There are two task:

1. On the bases of the accelarated tests data, to find the mean values of time of reliable operation, without failure $\bar{\tau}$ and the corresponding optimal approximation constants $\bar{a}$, $\bar{b}$, $\bar{c}$:

$$\bar{\tau} = \exp(\bar{a}\,t + \bar{b}\,U + \bar{c}) \qquad (12.4)$$

2. On the bases of the accelarated tests data, to find the values of time of reliable operation τ^* with in advance given probability and the corresponding optimal approximation constants a^*, b^*, c^*:

$$\tau^* = \exp(a^*t + b^*U + c^*) \qquad (12.5)$$

For the determination of the function (12.5) it is necessary the law of distribution of the stochastic variable τ to be known. In this chapter is accepted that the distribution is normal, because it is so in the most cases.

The theoretical results of the accelerated tests are shown in Table 12.1. For each combination of values of t and U, reliability tests are performed with k= 1,2...l$_{ij}$ samples. The number of samples l$_{ij}$ should be at least 35, but preferably 100, when not only the mean value $\bar{\tau}$, but also is necessary to find the values of time of reliable operation τ^* [8]. Also preferably the number of samples l$_{ij}$ should be approximately the same for all combinations of i and j. To obtain good approximation it is not necessary the number of n and m to be greater than 5 and to increase unnecessary the number of samples. They should be at least 3.

Table 12.1 Theoretical results of the accelerated tests

t	U_1	U_2	.....	U_j	....	U_m
t_1	$\tau_{11}^{(k)}$	$\tau_{12}^{(k)}$	.....	.....	.....	$\tau_{1m}^{(k)}$
t_2	$\tau_{21}^{(k)}$	$\tau_{22}^{(k)}$	.....	....	....	$\tau_{2m}^{(k)}$
.....	....	......	.....	.....	.....	......
t_i	....	....	.....	$\tau_{ij}^{(k)}$	.....	......
.....	.....	.....	.....	.....	.....	.....
t_n	$\tau_{n1}^{(k)}$	$\tau_{n2}^{(k)}$	....	....	.....	$\tau_{nm}^{(k)}$

12.2. Mathematical calculations of the results of the accelerated reliability tests

The mean value $\overline{\tau}_{ij}$ for each combination of i and j is calculated applying the formula:

$$\overline{\tau}_{ij} = \frac{1}{l_{ij}} \sum_{k=1}^{l_{ij}} \tau_{ij}^{(k)} \qquad (12.6)$$

Then for each combination of i and j is calculated the mean square deviation:

$$\sigma_{ij} = \left\{ \frac{1}{l_{ij}-1} \sum_{k=1}^{l_{ij}} (\tau_{ij}^{(k)} - \overline{\tau}_{ij})^2 \right\}^{1/2} \qquad (12.7)$$

and the work without failure with given probability:

$$\tau_{ij}^{*} = \overline{\tau}_{ij} - u_p \cdot \sigma_{ij}, \qquad (12.8)$$

where u_p is quantile of the normal distribution with given probability of work without failure. For example when $u_p=2$ the probability of work without failure in the interval $[0, \tau_{ij}{}^*]$ is 0.95. In this way the matrices $[\bar{\tau}_{ij}]$ and $[\tau_{ij}{}^*]$ are calculated. On the bases of these matrices of experimental data the optimal values of the constants $\bar{a}, \bar{b}, \bar{c}, a^*, b^*, c^*$ of the analytical approximations (12.4), (12.5) are found, seeking maximal closeness between the experimental data and the analytical approximation.

$$\left\| [\ln \exp(\bar{a}\, t_i + \bar{b}\, U_j + \bar{c})] - [\ln \bar{\tau}_{ij}] \right\| = \min \qquad (12.9)$$

$$\left\| [\ln \exp(a^*\, t_i + b^*\, U_j + c^*)] - [\ln \tau_{ij}{}^*] \right\| = \min \qquad (12.10)$$

The closeness is sought between the logarithms of the matrices, because in this case the task becomes linear. Of cause the solution in this case will be suboptimal. If an Euclid norm is applied then (12.9) and (12.10) can be written as:

$$\left\{ \sum_{i=1}^{n} \sum_{j=1}^{m} (\ln \bar{\tau}_{ij} - \bar{c} - \bar{a}\, t_i - \bar{b}\, U_j)^2 \right\}^{1/2} = \min \qquad (12.11)$$

$$\left\{ \sum_{i=1}^{n} \sum_{j=1}^{m} (\ln \tau_{ij}{}^* - c^* - a^* t_i - b^* U_j)^2 \right\}^{1/2} = \min \qquad (12.12)$$

The optimal values of $\bar{a}, \bar{b}, \bar{c}, a^*, b^*, c^*$ are found minimizing (11), (12) by taking partial derivatives of (12.11), (12.12) with respect to the unknown optimal values of the constants. The result is two linear systems:

$$\sum_{i=1}^{n} \sum_{j=1}^{m} t_i(\ln \bar{\tau}_{ij} - \bar{c} - \bar{a}\, t_i - \bar{b}\, U_j) = 0$$

$$\sum_{i=1}^{n} \sum_{j=1}^{m} (\ln \bar{\tau}_{ij} - \bar{c} - \bar{a}\, t_i - \bar{b}\, U_j) = 0 \qquad (12.13)$$

$$\sum_{i=1}^{n} \sum_{j=1}^{m} U_j(\ln \bar{\tau}_{ij} - \bar{c} - \bar{a}\, t_i - \bar{b}\, U_j) = 0$$

$$\sum_{i=1}^{n} \sum_{j=1}^{m} t_i(\ln \tau_{ij}^* - c^* - a^*t_i - b^*U_j)=0$$

$$\sum_{i=1}^{n} \sum_{j=1}^{m} (\ln \tau_{ij}^* - c^* - a^*t_i - b^*U_j)=0 \qquad (12.14)$$

$$\sum_{i=1}^{n} \sum_{j=1}^{m} U_j(\ln \tau_{ij}^* - c^* - a^*t_i - b^*U_j)=0$$

The calculated optimal values of $\bar{a}$, $\bar{b}$, $\bar{c}$, a^*, b^*, c^* should be replaced in the approximation functions (12.4), (12.5) and after that it is possible to determine $\bar{\tau}$ and τ^* for normal working conditions with given environmental factor t and criterion U.

The calculation of $\bar{a}$, $\bar{b}$, $\bar{c}$, a^*, b^*, c^* can be done applying the algorithm shown in the Fig.12.1.

REFERENCES

[1] N. Tenev, A. Krumov "Algorithm and program for accelerated reliability tests", Journal "Electrical industry and instruments" /in Bulgarian/, No.11, 1984, pp.4-7.

[2] Chan, H. "Accelerated Stress Testing Handbook: Guide for Achieving Quality Products", Publisher: Wiley-IEEE Press, Pages: 300 -307, Edition : 1, Copyright Year : 2001, ISBN : 9780470544051.

[3] Biernat J. , Jarnicki J. , Kaplon K., Kuras A., Anders G.J. "Reliability considerations in accelerated life testing of electrical insulation with generalized life distribution function", Power Systems, IEEE Transactions on, May 1992, Volume: 7, Issue: 2, Page(s): 656 – 664.

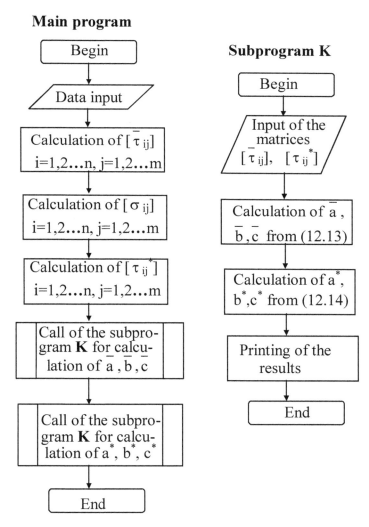

Main program

Begin

Data input

Calculation of $[\bar{\tau}_{ij}]$
$i=1,2\ldots n, j=1,2\ldots m$

Calculation of $[\sigma_{ij}]$
$i=1,2\ldots n, j=1,2\ldots m$

Calculation of $[\tau_{ij}^{*}]$
$i=1,2\ldots n, j=1,2\ldots m$

Call of the subprogram **K** for calculation of $\bar{a}, \bar{b}, \bar{c}$

Call of the subprogram **K** for calculation of a^{*}, b^{*}, c^{*}

End

Subprogram K

Begin

Input of the matrices
$[\bar{\tau}_{ij}], [\tau_{ij}^{*}]$

Calculation of $\bar{a}, \bar{b}, \bar{c}$ from (12.13)

Calculation of a^{*}, b^{*}, c^{*} from (12.14)

Printing of the results

End

Fig.12.1. Algorithm for accelerated reliability testing

[4] Sheu Bing J.; Hsu Wen-jay; Tyree Vance C. "Reliability assurance of application-specific microelectronic circuits", Reliability and Maintainability Symposium, 1990, Proceedings., 23-25 Jan, 1990, Page(s): 381 – 388.

[5] Heinen, Gail Gail; Schroen, Walter H.; Edwards, Darvin R.; Wilson, Arthur M.; Stierman, Roger J.; Lamson, Michael A. "Multichip Assembly With Flipped Integrated Circuits", Components, Hybrids, and Manufacturing Technology, IEEE Transactions on, Date of Publication: Dec 1989, Volume: 12, Issue: 4, Pages: 650 – 657.

[6] Kawai, Michifumi; Harada, Masahide; Andou, Akihiro; Yamada, Osamu; Satoh, Ryouhei; Netsu, Toshitada "Highly Accurate Design of Thermal Fatigue Life for Flipchip Joint", Electronic Components And Technology Conference, 1996. Proceedings., Date of Conference: 28-31 May, 1996, Pages: 1196 – 1201.

[7] Chan, H. Anthony "Accelerated stress testing for both hardware and software", Reliability And Maintainability, 2004 Annual Symposium – Rams, Date of Conference:2004, Pages: 346 – 351.

[8] Dostupov B. G. "Statistical methods in the design of nonlinear systems of automatic control"/in Russian/, Mashinostroenie, Moscow, 1970.

ABOUT THE AUTHOR

RESUME

of Associate Prof. Assen V. Krumov, Ph.D.

I was born in Plovdiv, Bulgaria. My school years I spent in Plovdiv and from 1960 I followed my studies at the Technical University in Sofia. Due to my excellent marks in 1962 I was elected to continue my education on a government grant in the Moscow Power Engineering Institute. There I received the degree of electrical engineer (equivalent to master degree) in 1966.

At this time I began my career at the Institute of Electrical Industry in Sofia as a research associate, at first at the high voltage test laboratory and after that (from 1970) at the computer department, where I worked as an application programmer in the area of computer modeling of electrical devices. In 1976 I became chief of the computer department and in 1981- senior research associate of computer aided electrical engineering.

I received my doctorate degree of theoretical electrotechnics from the Technical University of Sofia in

1976. The title of the dissertation was "Stochastic analysis of transient processes in the electrical systems".

Since 1989 I am associate professor of computer science at the Higher School of Transport in Sofia.

I am coauthor of three books, 100 scientific papers (25 in foreign journals or proceedings), 7 inventor's certificates and many technical reports in the following areas:
a) computer aided engineering;
b) embedded systems;
c) software and hardware;
d) analytical and computer modeling of dynamic systems;
e) electrotechnics

The full list of publications is in:
http://www.angelfire.com/space/assenkrumov/publist.html)
I have developed many software programs and have taken part in the design of many electrical devices with significant and well documented economic and technical results.

I am senior member of IEEE, of Computer society, Control system society.

I am included in the 2006-2007 Edition of Who's Who in Science and Engineering and in many other bibliographic editions.

Assoc. Prof. A. Krumov, Ph.D.

E-mail: assenkrumov@hotmail.com